Fatherly
Business
Conversations

Concepts and Systems You Don't
Necessarily Learn in College but Serve
You Well the Rest of Your Business Life

BOB PETTINELLI

Pettinelli Publishing

To all the teachers, especially the business teachers in this world, please know that commerce as we know it would grind to a halt if not for your dedication to the profession you so admirably serve.

Thank you!

A special thanks and appreciation to two dedicated teachers I am proud to know and love: Jane Scura, Ph.D. for your friendship, inspiration, guidance and tolerance and your best friend, my best friend, and my wife, Chris for just about everything else.

Never stop teaching.

TXu001984433
No part of this book may be distributed, reproduced or transmitted
in any form or by any means without prior written permission by
Pettinelli Publishing. bopett@hotmail.com, West Chester, PA

Editor: Mike Valentino, Salisbury, MA

Photo: Micduff Photography, Broomall, PA

Cover Design: Rick Holland, Vision Press, Tillson, NY

Copyediting, Interior Design, Index: Adept Content Solutions,
Urbana, IL

Library of Congress Control Number: 2016903394

Library of Congress Cataloging–in–Publication Data
PETTINELLI, Bob, author
Includes bibliographical reference and index

ISBN 978-0-9973554-0-6 (paperback)
ISBN 978-0-9973554-1-3 (eBook)

10 9 8 7 6 5 4 3 2 1

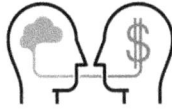

Contents

Keys to Individual Success

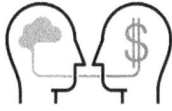

Competencies

About the Author

Bob Pettinelli is a sales, marketing, training, recruiting, and management consulting professional with a quantifiable record of increasing sales, productivity, and market share for large and small companies alike. Bob's insight spans both the corporate universe as well as the entrepreneurial space. He spent twenty-eight years with major, international companies and has been self-employed as a consultant, business owner, and distributor. Bob has held such corporate positions as Sales Director, Director of Trade Marketing, and Director of Sales Learning Systems—all for Fortune 10 companies.

Bob's Big 4 consulting assignments centered on developing Customer Relationship Management initiatives in the telecom industry. He also provided process evaluation, testing methodologies, database marketing re-engineering, and numerous sales mapping and benchmarking studies for communications companies. Additionally, he led visioning, leadership, and change management initiatives for consumer products companies and re-engineered the go-to market strategy for the country's largest franchised recruiting company.

The industries in which Bob has hands-on experience include consumer packaged goods, banking, franchising, retail food marketing, telecommunications, and consulting, executive recruiting, and advertising specialties.

Bob met his wife Christine at Mercyhurst University in Erie, Pennsylvania. He received a BA in Business, and Chris holds dual degrees in Elementary and Special Education. They currently reside in West Chester, Pennsylvania. Their three sons are working in different business verticals holding current titles of Vice President of Sales for a major international consumer package goods company; Internal Consultant, Executive Compensation and Planning for an international pharma company; and Manager World Wide Insurance and Risk Management for a global foodservice provider.

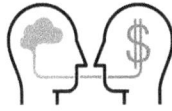

Prologue

*"In the business world, everyone is paid in two coins:
cash and experience. Take the experience first;
the cash will come later."*

Harold Geneen

Our family's kitchen table was the best classroom I ever had. My parents talked about their business, a small neighborhood Italian deli, endlessly. Our family (my parents, my slightly older brother, and I) worked together, ate together, went to church together—heck, we were a family; we also were in business together.

Mom had a tenth-grade education, and Pop graduated from high school; together they made a go of it—and by sheer osmosis their efforts shaped my future too. No, they didn't teach me about the essential elements of running a business—land, labor, capital, and entrepreneurial ability—which I learned later in business classes. What I did grasp, however, was crucial, as *little did I know* that these lessons would act as a base line to understand the collegial aspects of a business education; the lessons served as invaluable perspective for learning later on.

Yes, at the breakfast table I understood common sense relative to customer service, and that putting something on sale helped to attract new customers and retain your old ones too. There was no break-even analysis being discussed, yet I learned how to save money, if there was any leftover, on payday Fridays by putting excess cash in the business bank account. In business school they call it "plowing profits back into the business," perhaps even "retained earnings." Pop didn't have a customer service department and never heard of retained earnings, but his customers kept coming back, and he always had a dollar in his pocket. Pop knew how to smile while he worked, and he was always glad to get through another week, careful to sketch out the activities ahead, never even realizing that he'd inadvertently mastered the art of business planning. He was also adept at hiring and scheduling, not knowing he was the HR department—whoever heard of such a thing? Pop was the CEO—three letters he'd never put together. Though educationally challenged by today's standards, my parents were smart people in their own right. Both of them surpassed their parents' scholastic endeavors, low bars notwithstanding. They didn't know it was called continuous improvement.

Our endless conversations at the kitchen table—which ran the gamut from advertising to taxes and everything in between—gave me the invaluable gift called "perspective." I could see and feel real agony and pain when business was soft. It hurt my parents, and I felt it too. The Grim Reaper was always just a few bad days away. When times were good, though, I could see my parents' excitement and enjoyed the new baseball glove that came with it. Their success also provided a college education for me, an accomplishment steeped in redemption that my parents took great pride in. This was especially important to my father, who had always wanted to go to college but never had a chance to.

The many years of listening to my parents' unbridled, unfiltered opinions based on real-life business circumstances and nothing else have proven to be invaluable. Make it a point to find great teachers in your own life. I'm talking about business elders who are hardworking people living in the real world every day, actually doing the things that modern-day professors theoretically teach about. Lectures may be fine and good, but I'm talking about people who are planning business without writing business plans. They are creating what marketing is all about while never having heard of the concept. They are conducting market research by walking down the street to check out the competition. They do payroll on the back of a paper sack; they have no idea what EBITDA is, but they somehow get the numbers to the accountant to pay their taxes. They wake up and go to sleep thinking about their business. They are all in in the game of life and of business, and fortunately for me, I grew up listening to two of the best of them talking about it—all of it—all the time.

• • •

Years later, while a management consultant, I came to learn and understand a concept called gap analysis, which bills billions of dollars annually due to its relative importance to business growth. In a nutshell, here's the gist of it: knowing where to go without knowing where you came from is simply a recipe for disaster. Understanding the base line is valuable and even more meaningful than knowing where you want to go, for it exposes all the warts. The stuff in between is the gap analysis, the bridge connecting the past to the future. It forms the basis for the plan to move forward, which, when executed, leads to a sustainable competitive advantage (SCA) that all businesses seek. In fact, it's almost pointless to be in business otherwise. What every business needs is an enduring, preeminent capacity to outperform competitors by using intrinsic attributes and capabilities that are difficult to duplicate. Think about what your business, and you personally, can bring to the table that nobody else can. That is your competitive advantage; identify it, use it every single day, and let it grow so strong that it becomes unstoppable.

The "gap" between the kitchen table and management consulting lies in principled, disciplined, and foundational concepts that, when understood, mastered, and consistently applied, lead to success in every walk of life. This inherent gap is all but eliminated by the accumulation of the core operating principles presented in this book.

• • •

That kitchen table is your base line. For as you will hear, your business life is all about knowing what matters. The end game is really all about enjoying the process of getting to the finish line. In between it's all about expending energy while focused on a task. It's about getting better from making critical decisions and growing from being good at what you do to becoming competent at what you lead others to do. It is feeling success because you can think in three dimensions at once, knowing full well you are grounded in lasting principles; it's not a mode of trial and error but of trial and triumph. Think of it as a process, a system of sorts where you learn from everyone and everything and even from the unexpected—just the way it happens at the kitchen table.

All you have to do to be successful is listen to and apply what others have learned. Take what you like from the lessons in this book and build upon them and let the "human sponge" (your ears and your willingness to listen) do its thing for you. You might think that because you were born with a brain that you can do anything—and maybe you can—but let's be clear: the brain doesn't come with instructions. Not only that, but it can also tune out and turn off. Ears, on the other hand, are always "on" and therefore working for you. Putting them to work is somewhat routine, and in your formative business years all you need to do to learn is listen; no brain work is required.

You will discover as you continue reading that there are eight attributes that will serve you well in the business world and in life in general. Some of them may sound very simple, but don't let that fool you. As you delve more deeply into this book, it will start becoming clear to you that these attributes are indispensable. Every person who has become a success uses them, not in the form of this exact list, but the basics of these eight attributes are always in place for those who get ahead of the game and stay there:

1. Master something; be principled; focus on focusing.

2. Be truly customer centric in the business world, but first become egocentric in your personal world.

3. You need not be better than anybody else—just be better tomorrow. Or put another way: "If you could have a thought, what would it be?"

4. Think and converse in business terms and in business settings by behaving *"businessorally"*; that is, know how to think and converse in business terms and in business settings.

5. Have a business plan in your pocket at all times.

6. Planning without execution is merely an exercise in futility.

7. Work toward securing a sustainable competitive advantage for your business unit; develop a personal sustainable indispensable competency or two for yourself.

8. When it comes to personal and perpetual success, adopt a sense of urgency.

Think of the eight attributes as what you need to do to become the business go-to guy. Think of them as the answers to the questions of what really matters in the context of managing a career. Align yourself with these eight pain-relieving attributes to remain in a state of purposeful posture. A lot of this probably isn't making too much sense to you right now, but by the time you finish reading this book, my hope is that it will already be starting to become second nature to you.

And that is what you will find in the pages that follow. I talk about experiences and speak *"businessorally"* so you can relate to what you must do in order to tackle the challenges of both business and life. By this I mean the kind of language you hear all the time in the business world, which is often quite different from the language of everyday life. Heed advice from the past president of a multinational conglomerate, ITT when the eminent Harold Geneen exults, "experience trumps cash," knowing full well the latter will come to those deserving of its just reward.

So, my fatherly advice:

Grab a cup of coffee, relax at the kitchen table, and for a change let your ears read for you because this is the stuff you don't necessarily learn in college, but it will no doubt serve you well the rest of your business life.

1

The Conversation Unspoken

"Silence is one of the great arts of conversation."

Marcus Tullius Cicero

I was just a young up-and-coming soldier in the business army of a Fortune 10 company when it struck me: I knew nothing. It all started with a conversation I didn't know I was about to have with a man I barely knew. I remembered seeing him in the annual report—his picture was striking. He had a very impressive title complete with initials after his name.

The setting was New York City, and as fate would have it, while attending a breakfast meeting in the Big Apple, I simply entered an elevator. The express elevator stopped to pick me up on the sixtieth floor, and I stepped in. With a nod and an obligatory "morning" accompanied by a perfunctory smile, I took my spot to the left of the sole occupant in the eight-foot-by-ten-foot mirrored car.

Fatherly Business Conversations

Then it happened. In a flash I was reduced to a mere business neophyte by the voice behind his steely grey eyes when he simply asked, "How's business?"

In a New York second my heart dropped while my oatmeal churned up from my stomach and thankfully lodged in my throat. I was paralyzed, and then I blinked, signaling my brain that I was still alive; *Now what?*

With sour oatmeal dripping from the corner of my mouth I uttered, "*Good*" as his gaze penetrated right through my eyes and straight to my brain. Without a spoken word he was asking, "If you could have a thought what would it be?"

There were only fifty-nine floors to go. It was 6:34 A.M.; would my career be over by lunch time? Without either of us saying another word, we both knew I had screwed up royally. It was my big chance to score—and I fumbled the ball like a klutz!

I wish I could tell you that at that point I said something that catapulted me to the executive suite, but I cannot. I didn't vomit, either. However, the business gods shined on me that day as I farted—loudly, and the laughter lasted fifty-nine seconds. Well, I don't know if it was actually fifty-nine seconds, but I'm certain my face was red for the whole time. We both scurried out of the car, me hoping that no one would link us to the fumes left behind and him presumably the same. Not exactly the lasting impression I wanted to leave; however, I did survive the toughest sixty seconds of my business life.

Most people, I guess, would simply move on telling the funny story along the way. Not me. No, somehow my makeup allows for reflection via an ingrained business strategy I developed early on in my career. The nightly tactic was to go over each day's events looking for any kind of learning that would help me grow. That night I learned a few things, paramount among them that farts are not only funny—and truly a life saver, but that it would be wise to have a business plan in my pocket at all times. You never know when you may be put on the spot like I was, and then you'll thank me.

Stocking your business war chest with sound principles and understanding core concepts almost guarantee a rewarding career. After all, flatulence will only take you so far.

If only I knew back then what I was about to learn over the next few decades while in that elevator! Trust me, I would look good in a New York City penthouse.

It was an opportunity wasted, but I discovered perspective and prayed for redemption.

• • •

To my father, Pop, the top three conversations we enjoyed centered on sports, politics, and business. If the list was just business we talked about staying current, getting better, and growing the business.

So, my fatherly advice:

- Anticipate the next fork in the road. Get out ahead of it. Learn to hit the curve ball. Be prepared when entering an elevator.

- Work smarter and plan on being successful. Stay ahead of the pack.

- Build a foundation for yourself and your family. Know what matters to you. Use your brain, even when it hurts. Understand and practice the concepts that follow in this book.

Let's converse about what matters; continuously improving yourself, thinking constantly and *businessorally,* being competent while thankfully working and being successful, and understanding the concept of "trial and triumph" (which I will explain shortly) while using the lost art of conversation. In business, that means getting straight to the point. Forget small talk and trying to sound clever. That always backfires, and you end up regretting it. Say exactly what you mean right from the start, frankly, factually, and articulately, and never look back.

2

What Matters
Simply Stated

"Simple can be harder than complex: You have to work hard to get your thinking clean to make it simple. But it's worth it in the end as once you get there, you can move mountains."

Steve Jobs

Pop's sage advice first and foremost was to understand what matters. Let's talk about it.

THE SIMPLICITY OF MATTER. If I asked what is important to you, it would be the same as asking what matters to you. Whatever it is that gives life not only meaning, but the many flavors of pure joy that makes it worth living in the first place—that's what matters when you come right down to it. Does it have to be something of major importance to everyone in the world, like some profound astronomical event that we all can witness or a huge holiday that entices the whole world? No. Not at all. It's what matters to you as an individual that's important.

There's one problem, though. You will easily lose sight of the little things in life that truly do matter, precisely because they are so small. Far too often we let the perceptions of others set the agenda for our own minds. Why not think for yourself instead? What is important to somebody else might mean less than nothing to you and vice versa. Isn't it great being an individual? If the same things mattered to all of us, in the exact same measure, this world would be a pretty boring place.

We could try making a list of what matters, but it would only be to illustrate that a truly inclusive list would literally be endless. The possibilities are as wide as your imagination and as deep as your heart's desires. But let's take a shot at it anyway.

- Things like simple traditions, and not necessarily Thanksgiving dinner but, "It smells like Sunday" matters to anyone born to a tomato sauce–making Italian family.

- Things like the sounds of spring are really the always fun nattering of kids playing baseball after a long winter season.

- Things like having your breath taken from you when catching a glimpse of a special her . . . need I say more?

- Things like any of Leo Buscaglia's preaching's, such as hugging a tree matters.

- Things like a grandson's second birthday party—that matters greatly.

- Things like a little girl seeing the globe for the first time and wondering just how all this happened.

Why do these things matter? Because these simple, small things enrich your life unlike money, status, station in life, or anything else and provide the calm in your personal storm;

they energize without stimulants, and most importantly they define why you are alive. Without these simple things the big, more complex things in life dominate your being and rob you of a sense different than smell, sound, and touch. They provide the rock from which you are tethered—the compass that always points not necessarily north but in the right direction—and they allow simple things to creep back into your life while providing the one vitamin that makes it worth living and it is called . . . wait for it. . . *perspective.*

Yes, perspective is the magic elixir (and it's even free!) that somehow disappears from your diet. Perspective is the missing ingredient in the formula for true reasoning as we constantly strive to recapture the innocence we enjoyed at the moment of our birth—unencumbered, reactionary, needy, and full of wonderment without prejudice, without bad thoughts, and with all the hope the universe can muster. The insatiable thirst for a return to that moment swims around in our consciousness constantly, though it's hardly ever noticed. It is only felt in moments that are somewhat unexpected, quasi surreal, and delightfully ingested. They instantly provide a calmness not found in any other endeavor we engage in—for a fleeting small amount of time everything is alright, everything is in place, the orbits align, and—quite literally—nothing else matters.

Better yet, it's a respite from what has become our norm—the routine, mundane agenda of doing things we have come to know as important until we smell the sauce cooking, hear the crack of the bat, see a sneak peek of her silhouette and the glistening candle in front of the circular ruby lips of a beautiful child having the most fun in the world blowing on flickering blue and yellow wisps of air we call birthday candles. Of course, we're not consciously thinking of the significance of any of this. Not for a single moment. That would ruin it. We're too busy simply enjoying it. The whole thing happens so naturally we barely even notice it, and that's OK because deep down inside you know darn well that it sure does matter. That is why our blood pressure retreats, our breathing is effortless, and our general well-being equates to a Rocky Mountain high.

Perspective aligns with redemption as another elusive release in our search for true meaning. Redemption matters because it frees us from the shackles that we mostly place upon ourselves. Since they are self-imposed we seldom think to free ourselves from the grip of senseless activities. In other words, it's impossible to screw things up so badly that you can never fix them. But first you have to acknowledge that redemption is always there, if only you are willing to claim it and embrace it. Make it your own.

Of course, you can't practice perspective or redemption, and you really can't learn them either. Perspective is acquired, and redemption is soulful, making both liberators free yet rich, fleeting yet long lasting, necessary yet luxurious. Their invaluable gift is to keep reminding us that the little things really do matter. If not, we would run in a straight line without hope for new beginnings, we would heap sorrow upon sorrow without the chance to make things better, and the little girl's globe would be as flat as a pancake without the wonderment that really matters.

• • •

So how does all this matter in the larger scope of the business world?

One need only have the all-too-occasional stiff neck or the phantom leg cramp or the upshot migraine headache to stake out membership in the inexorably, inescapably, and unavoidably real corporate club of modern day business. Yes, totally unavoidable if you want to secure the means for an enriched life. Yes, inescapable if you desire to be challenged beyond your wildest imaginings. And yes, inexorable because it is inevitable that all of your business life will find you embroiled in a constant state of "what the heck!" as time after time you will feel like the mole in the Whack-A-Mole game. Trust me, it is worse than knee replacement surgery, a root canal, and a kidney stone attack all together—and I have had all three. This place called corporate life is unknown to the average person. It is a jungle, pure and simple. But if navigated successfully you can expect plenty of rewards. When you really think about it, there is no other place that you can be or will want to be but in something that is organic and dynamic, multi-faceted, and ever changing all the while providing you the means to live your life the best way you see fit.

So, the question becomes: how do you navigate this work-place jungle in which you need so very much to flourish?

The following chapters will provide a glimpse into what it takes to successfully traverse the real world of business. When you understand and incorporate these half-dozen concepts into your daily routine, they will become your guidebook for business navigation. The chapters are a foundational approach to life and business, as I feel that both are intertwined: you can't have one without the other. In fact, one sets up the other. But first, you must reflect and figure out what really matters to you. Things that matter allow you to reach for the brass ring. They are like an energy drink and aspirin all rolled up into one.

By understanding these "things not necessarily learned in college" you will get more than you can imagine in terms of principled, foundational building blocks. Each of them is geared to your business growth in particular and ultimately to your success and happiness in the overall game of life in general.

Apple's inventor, marketer, co-founder, and chairman Steve Jobs intimated that simple ideas can move mountains. This chapter simply expounds on what really matters in life to some people. To me, it is all about the sheer joy of watching my grandson blowing out candles and having a blast doing it. If you can't see perspective in this chapter then re-read it and get re-focused as the remaining chapters relate to the business world you must navigate so that the essence of life really matters to you and your family. Knowing what matters is not only foundational but mandatory, for without it your rudderless trek through life will result in mediocrity at best. I say clear your head of complex matters and simply endeavor to move more mountains!

• • •

To my father, Pop, the top three things that mattered to him were family, business and golf. To his last breath, these stayed the same.

So, my fatherly advice:

- Name your top three personal things that really matter.
- Name your top three business things that really matter.
- Focus on the simple things first.
- Rid yourself of all possible angst.
- What have you witnessed recently that gave you perspective?
- What can you do in the next week to give you redemption?
- Name five things outside of work that mattered to you in the last month. Say them again and *smile*!

Repeat this series of questions once a month! Start cultivating perspective and redemption and find out what really matters to you.

Let's converse about continuously improving yourself, thinking constantly and businessorally—being competent while thankfully working and being successful, and understanding the concept of trial and triumph while using the art of conversation to attain lofty goals in your business life.

3

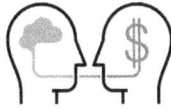

Improving Continuously
The Constant Gaze of Ha?

"You can tell whether a man is clever by his answers. You can tell whether a man is wise by his questions."

Naguib Mahfouz

Pop's sagacity included anticipating the next fork in the road. He always said to get out ahead of it. Little did I know there was a forked road in an eight foot by ten foot elevator car, and I was in no way ahead of it! I wasn't even abreast of it. Let's talk about how you might navigate that.

CONTINUOUS IMPROVEMENT. If you are looking for a guiding principle to incorporate into your daily life, keep in mind that the concept of continuous improvement (CI), when fully understood, becomes a self-fulfilling replenishing idea machine!

This powerful concept often induces an almost hypnotic state of inquisitiveness that allows you to be a perpetual first grader who sees the globe for the first time and wonders just how big the world is. Imagine living in a world where you constantly ask questions. Since the questions need answers, it forces you to do more thinking than if the question had never been posed in the first place. Never asking questions is just plain foolish, and maybe even worse is, when you think you have the answer, to sit back and rest on your laurels, thinking all is well forever. If we were all like that mankind's progress would stand still. The invention of the wheel would be about as far as we'd get, if we were lucky.

Surviving—forget prospering—in this state seems challenging enough, yet I say, why not? I say that living in the CI state is living with all the answers as answering is easier than questioning even though the common belief says otherwise.

Why, you ask (there you go, day one living in the CI state), can answering be easier than questioning? Because there will always be more questions than answers. If not, mankind morphs into oblivion as Armageddon sets in. How can the universe sustain itself if we stop trying to understand ourselves? How can we explore the moon if we stop figuring out how we get there? Does this matter? Will having ample perspective enhance the CI conundrum? Is CI just asking questions?

So, just what is the thing called continuous improvement? Is it merely a corporate buzzword just like "paradigm" was in the 1990s? Is it a process like six sigma, or perhaps a self-fulfilling prophecy? Is it real or imagined; does it have a real basis in logic and operation or is it just plain propaganda? Does it matter; is it relevant; does it have a sense of perspective/redemption about it?

First, let's look at what CI might be and a good example is what a well-intentioned Southern state education society (Florida

Department of Education) claims it is: "Continuous improvement is a way of work where data about the impact of ongoing practices is used to improve and refine those practices." That sounds more like a mission statement from the corporate world of the 1980s that used to be proudly displayed in waiting rooms and entryways across the land not so many years ago. However, the essence of CI is in the definition, at least in part, as the word improvement is central to the process and outcome of CI principles. I'd give the Florida Department of Education a B-.

A better example comes from the world of finance where Clarence W. Barron, a nineteenth century president of Dow Jones & Company and arguably the founder of modern financial journalism profoundly stated what you would think should be painfully obvious: "Everything can be improved." The difference between the two definitions, besides brevity versus mumbo jumbo, is that one is simple, as it does not have to be read and reread to be understood. The constant is the theme of improvement, but neither tells *how* to improve (well, not in any practical detail), nor do they define the continuous part of continuous improvement. Barron's declaration merits a B+.

Continuous, on the other hand is also a simple idea. Always, never ending, and all the time come to mind. So do repeat, recur, and regular. This leads to another definition, and this time it is from Japan and more aptly Japan's need to rebuild their country after World War Two. In so doing, they sought "good change" or *Kaizen*, meaning continuous improvement, as the concept was really born out of necessity. In essence, the country adopted this way of life as a long-term approach to work that systematically sought to achieve small, incremental process changes in order to improve efficiency and quality of Japanese living. The Kaizen approach surely incorporates the continuous portion of the concept, and now we are closer to the true meaning of continuous improvement. Some might say that since their industry was flattened by the Allied strategic bombing campaign during the war, that not only was Kaizen responsible for Japan's success but they were able to rebuild "from the ground up," starting from scratch using the newest techniques to build new assembly lines and new production techniques.

Interestingly enough, it is an American, Dr. W. Edwards Deming, who is actually credited as the founder of the Kaizen philosophy. Deming was recruited to Japan to assist the county in its epic post–World War Two do-over. Deming authored his book *Out of Crisis* as a philosophic tell-all on continuous improvement and spells out fourteen principles covering everything from fear to leadership. He taught about the relationships of consistency, training, self-improvement, and ultimate transformation, thus ensuring continuous improvement.

So good was Deming's philosophy that in a sense he showed the Japanese how to think about the process of lifting its society into the twentieth century. Eventually, Japan became a major world power once again. Deming incorporated the Kaizen way, and in an effort to realize real change, the concept became the responsibility of every Japanese citizen. This *responsibility* is the missing link that most in our modern society do not accept or even realize as it matters not to the non-thinkers, the takers, or the ill-informed among us. Maybe it takes a culture like Japan's with its dedication to responsibility to highlight this, but whatever it is, it makes CI a necessity. However, in adopting this responsible posture any person becomes a one percenter on this spinning globe of adventure, and isn't that a great place to be!

So, is CI all about asking questions? As you can see the answer is emphatically no! Just by using these few examples one can see that CI is much more than simply asking questions. Questions beget answers, answers beget more questions, and the cycle goes on and on ad infinitum until a permanent state of inquisitiveness sets in. It matters because this principle alters your state of being and allows for the concept of perspective to work its magic for you. Inherent in the process is the resultant and constant "perspective multiplier" where you not only get the answer but instantly realize there is another conundrum to ponder. In the end, the realization is that the CI process leads one to become more adroit in thinking, reasoning, anticipating, and planning, as well as organizing, collating, and remaining largely and naturally extremely inquisitive.

Yes, CI is far above the questions/answers routine; rather, it is all about the *process of getting there* that makes it a magical place to be. Understand that living CI is the ultimate goal, and once you get there, you see that you cannot stay there, just like it is impossible to run in place forever. While the merits of sweaty exercise are both physical and mental, the visceral routine of living CI is just as exhausting. With physical exercise you will eventually collapse, but with visceral exercise you will be forever invigorated. Moreover, since there is never a resting place for the CI subscribers, they perpetually ensure the planet continues on its axis, and all the world benefits from its existence.

And so, at the end of the day, I would say that continuous improvement is all about staying in the inquiry mode, as it will lead to ideas about what is practical and promote concepts that are doable. Most rewarding of all, it will place you into a permanent state of supreme wonderment and challenge and allow you to make a difference where difference is always mandated. Yes, continuous improvement when fully and unconsciously practiced will enhance the person, the organization and even the world. It will change everything that matters, especially the big things, and in fact, it is the only way things change . . . period.

• • •

How does this all work in the larger scope of the business world? Perhaps the real question is how can anyone think that day one of their business career will be the same as the last day of the thirtieth year or beyond? Do you really believe that once you secure a position that you are set for life? It is the fool who adopts the "entitlement philosophy," yet so many do. Yes "change" is evident but not so clear on day one. What is clearly evident (looking back) is how much you need to change to stay relevant, and becoming the agent of change is the essence of continuous improvement. Simply stated, change or get run over could be the motto of this concept named continuous improvement.

Almost anyone you know will be able to tell you stories about how they led change or fought change and to save face, how ultimately they embraced the eventual outcomes of change. For you see, it is human nature to criticize and revolt against another's idea (latent agenda), to challenge the status quo and rebel against their own personal paradigms of how the world should spin. That's why becoming comfortable and complacent is tantamount to corporate death.

Living continuously to improve one's position in life via hard work is the antidote for complacency. Think of it this way: why would a leader want a team full of mediocre albeit average performers if he is to win the competitive battle against the top players in their field? He wouldn't, and neither should you settle for anything less than the best you/they can offer. As you will see, you need not be better than anyone else . . . just be better tomorrow. This is a key learning point we will discuss in more detail later (Chapter 7). It will be crucial for your success in both business and in life.

Grinding toward this endless goal puts you in the "constant state of ha" and places you—yes, you—in the center of it all. Yes, to be truly customer centric in the business world you must first become egocentric in the personal world. It is all about you, your family, your community, and your world. By making yourself better, you make everything better. How-to books are good, very good indeed, for specific things that matter to you. Wouldn't it be great if all of the how-to books were in one place and at your fingertips? Well, they are! They are in your being, your make up, and your persona, and all they need to work is an igniter and that is you and only you. You need only to live in the *constant gaze of ha!*

What most co-workers will not tell you is how they came to the realization that change is a good thing, for most people do fight it, fearing the unknown and consequently living in a negative world. These nay-sayers are the obstructionists, the anti-Christs and the devil all in one. They hide behind false notions of change being the death knell of civilization, fearing they will be left out of something they perceive as an ulterior motive by someone with an idea. These potential corporate partners are obvious and obnoxious and are to be swiftly distanced from, as negativity is the single most despicable trait one can adopt, and in business it is a career stopper. Avoid these people like the plague and never fall prey to their disillusioned ideology.

Business history is full of examples of how continuous improvement shaped the financial world with nary a mention of the concept. Let's go back to Clarence W. Barron. Barron was renowned for pushing for deep scrutiny of corporate financial records and is thus considered the founder of modern financial journalism. Barron's personal credo, which he supposedly urged the *Wall Street Journal* to print and follow was "The *Wall Street Journal* must stand for what is best in Wall Street." In 1913, he gave testimony to the Massachusetts Public Service Commission regarding a slush fund held by the New Haven Railroad. In 1920 he investigated Charles Ponzi, inventor of the Ponzi scheme, for the *Boston Post*. His aggressive questioning and common-sense reasoning helped lead to Ponzi's arrest and conviction. There you see it: "His aggressive questioning and common sense reasoning" is the essence of continuous improvement, but who knew and really who cared? The takeaway is that by staying in the inquiry mode, Barron continually contributed to the entire world of finance, and to this day his continuous improvement posture positively affects each of us.

As smart as Barron was he may not have been aware that he was a devotee of CI. But he exuded it, lived it, practiced it—continuously—and one hundred years later is lauded for his application of it.

The aforementioned Dr. Deming is truly the poster boy for this wonderful concept. I suggest his book *Out of Crisis* to anyone who is in the business world, as conceptually most other processes and systems follow from his ideas. Although his slant is on the manufacturing process as seen in his published fourteen points of light, I have summarized his teachings here as the five core principles of the essence of continuous improvement for the masses:

- Create constancy of purpose towards improvement

- Adopt the new philosophy

- Improve constantly and forever

- Institute education and self-improvement

- Transformation is everyone's job

In the business world this is it. The end-all to end all—organic growth at its best and it's practically free.

This concept, if ingrained and practiced individually, will set you up for success as much as your college degree, your MBA, or your CPE credits, no matter the discipline. In fact, continuous improvement will augment your formal learnings like nothing else. It will assist you in all endeavors, for you will never run out of questions to your answers!

As famed Nobel Prize winner Naguib Mahfouz astutely proclaimed, "A wise man is known by his questions." So understand this continuous improvement concept; learn and incorporate it into your being, and practice it at all times. Most importantly live it, exemplify it, mentor it, and be amazed by it, for without it life will be simply exhausting and not exhilarating, and wouldn't that be a shame? And if you need a continuous improvement motto to live by, try this: "You need not be better than anybody else—just be better tomorrow." Or put another way, "If you could have a thought, what would it be?"

• • •

To my father, Pop, the top three things he tried to get better at were home improvements, golfing, and running his business.

So, my fatherly advice:

- Think about your top three personal improvement areas that really matter and how you might improve upon them.

- Think about your top three business improvement areas that really matter and how you might improve upon them.

- Remain relevant. Keep growing. Be decisive.

- Ask yourself, are you better today than yesterday?

- Are you questioning answers?

Let's converse about thinking constantly and *businessorally*, being competent while thankfully working and being successful; and understanding the concept of "trial and triumph" while using the art of conversation to attain lofty goals in your business life.

4

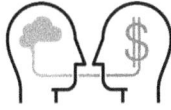

Thinking Critically
Thinking Businessorally

*"Five percent of the people think;
ten percent of the people think they think;
and the other eighty-five percent would rather die than think."*

Thomas A. Edison

Pop's intuition told him and, clairvoyantly, me to use the brain, even when it hurts. He knew nothing of the percentages Edison was talking about, but he lived in the world of the five percenters. Let's talk about how you can up your game.

CRITICAL THINKING. In life, I contend one gets to make four or five very critical decisions. I'm talking major, life-altering choices. Furthermore, a good percentage of your decisions will undoubtedly revolve around your work. "Thinking" is indeed critical to every aspect of life. So think, even when it hurts!

All business people need to know how to think and converse in business terms and in business settings, that is, *businessorally.* I am not talking return on assets, interest rates, market share, stock price, or anything like that. You will learn what is germane to your firm, your competitors, and your industry as well as shareholder and stakeholder preferences from your corporate mentors. But after that you are left to your own devices to *think* and ultimately make a difference.

This concept of *businessorally* is critical for so many reasons. You won't find it in any dictionary, but it's about entering into a business frame of mind every single day. While tough to define, I contend that the intangible, almost innate ability to think, speak and behave businessorally is the rare marriage of conversational intelligence with a demonstrated aptitude to grasp the essence of business challenges. It's getting to the kernel of an issue succinctly and proficiently, using constantly applied principles of conceptual thinking.

Let's delve into this businessorally thing so you too can master its tenets and be in a coveted position in all business discussions. A good place to start is by wrapping your mind around these three questions:

THREE QUESTIONS

1. What do you think about?

2. How do you think businessorally?

3. Just as importantly, how do you present what you are thinking about?

These three "things that matter" clearly emanate from your desire to make something better or fix a (potential) problem or find a better way/process. By some sort of order—your personal initiative or your supervisor's whim—you need to do something that ultimately affects the bottom line. Affecting the bottom line means to influence it.

ONE ANSWER

The continuous improvement element residing in me says, "Have a business plan, or at least some aspect of the business, *your* piece of it, in your pocket at all times." Yes, this is the answer to the questions posed about how and what to think about and present those thoughts *businessorally.* Adopting this posture will serve you well as you will always and forever *never be without* something important and impactful to do or say. Read that again and again to see the essence of this entire book, *The Things You Don't Necessarily Learn in College: have a business plan in your pocket at all times!*

Yes, you may learn about the elements of a business plan while in college and even write one in the business world, but once completed, 20XX ABCs of the XYZ Company, Volume 1, goes up on the shelf gathering dust, never again to be seen or acted upon, never to be read by anyone, never to have impact. It becomes a static piece of business history—an exercise in futility that is far too common.

Maybe a real life situation that one of my sons experienced will help to illustrate the point. It is sort of his "elevator moment"— or rather one of many such encounters he and you and I will be subjected to throughout our careers.

The situation: After a forty-minute pre-dawn ride to work, my VP son arrives at the parking lot to his office. Upon exiting the car he is approached by the division president, his boss's boss's boss, no less. With a commanding look and a stern voice the president asks the VP: "What did you sell yesterday, Bob?" No, "Hi, how are you?" Or "It's good to see you; how are the wife and kids?" It's simply the big guy squarely in "businessorally" mode. It's a fair question; after all the VP is in charge of sales for $50 million of revenue, and the big boss needs to know if he is going to make his $4 billion number.

After that encounter, the day was all downhill, right? Well, not exactly. After the exchange with the president, Bob, Jr. gets to his work space longing for that wake-up cup of coffee, and waiting for him is his boss's boss. Bob, Jr. begins to think it's going to be a tough day, just like yesterday and the day before! This divisional vice-president has obviously had a few cups of morning Joe as he tells Bob, Jr. that he has about thirty or so questions on the Convenience Channel business review he sent him last night and wants to go over them right now. "And, oh by the way, I see you met up with the big guy. How'd that go?"

Here within the first fifteen minutes at work—and even before that first sip of wake-up coffee—this young professional was shot at not once but twice. How'd he do? Did he survive? Is his career still intact? Just think, he hasn't even seen his boss yet! Oh, and three of his subordinates left messages looking for assistance on their business plans. Heck, it's not even 8 A.M., and it's only the first day of the new fiscal year!

I'm glad to report he did just fine with both encounters, and I can tell you how he internalized his feelings at those moments. His businessorally mode kicked in about two minutes after kissing his wife goodbye as his thoughts went to the day's challenges. He looks at them as opportunities so his mental preparation puts him into a purposeful posture mode of operation. In his mind, he turned the president's question into "how's business?" and astutely went into a verbal discourse about his successful trip with a new distributor. Sensing the answer must be swiftly orated, he top-lined the situation, disclosed that the big opportunity was met with an action plan that, if implemented, would result in orders totaling $2 million. He laid out the plan and his immediate next steps to the president's full understanding.

The president's reply was along the lines of an "atta-boy, keep up the good work" as he left to move on to different prey! Suffice it to say, Bob, Jr. was mentally prepared and ready for the questions with answers as he practices continuous improvement principles and applies critical thinking methods all the time.

Oh, and how about the boss's boss and the thirty questions? Bob, Jr. had the answers, as we all should, because his businessorally posture serves him well time and time again. It's all in a day's work. Are you positively and continually affecting business results like Bob, Jr.? Would you like to know the process Bob, Jr. applies on a continual basis?

Well, his idea is to know his business and every aspect of it by having a business plan in his pocket at all times. The ability to articulate it at a moment's notice is the indisputable skill. In so doing, he—and you, too—can establish an iterative process that ensures you're moving in the right direction—and not necessarily north! The critical thinking part is now done for you—it is part of you, and now you can concentrate on presenting those ideas to affect change or the bottom line or the outcome of an important business meeting. You will be the one who has a lasting effect on the outcome of the firm's results.

Hopefully you get the message: thinking, even when it hurts, is essential to success in the business world.

• • •

Before learning about the characteristics of the process, understand that thinking is very close to presenting in the business world as oftentimes you get little warning or time to say something important (as Bob, Jr. encountered). Thus, as a first step, having that organic plan at the forefront of your cerebral cortex is priority number one. Second, even with ample preparation, you will need to articulate elements or all of the plan at a moment's notice and at a critical time, like the impromptu meeting I had in the New York City elevator.

Presenting this plan in orderly fashion all while exhibiting clarity becomes an essential part of the entire process. Consider this thought, especially those of us not possessing an innate sales personality, that upon opening your mouth to present your plan you are in effect selling it. There is just no avoiding that.

And so the three-part process to accomplish a complete critical decision system—thinking, presenting and selling—need to be one in thought and ultimately in delivery. The central question becomes, how do you present your thoughts coherently? To do that you need to think in a certain way: the same way successful business leaders think! You would benefit from having etched into your thought process a template or system to plug into at any given time that will yield results time and time again. The system will allow for clarity and succinctness to ensure understanding and acceptance of concepts. It must be part of who you are—an expected contributor—at all times. This is the thought process that will set you apart from the pretenders; it's all about the system!

Thinking Critically

Introducing the Six-Step
Thinking/Presenting/Selling Process (TPS)

- THE FACTUAL SITUATION
- THE BIG QUESTION or BIG IDEA or BIG ISSUE(s)
- THE PLAN
- HOW THE PLAN WORKS
- HOW WE WILL MEASURE SUCCESS
- IMMEDIATE NEXT STEPS

• • •

THE SITUATION:

_____

_____

_____

_____

_____

_____

THE BIG QUESTION(s) or BIG IDEA(s) or BIG ISSUE(s):

_____

_____

_____

_____

_____

_____

_____

_____

THE PLAN(s):

_____

_____

_____

_____

_____

HOW THE PLAN(s) WORK:

_____

_____

_____

_____

_____

_____

HOW WE MEASURE SUCCESS(s):

_____

_____

_____

_____

_____

_____

_____

IMMEDIATE NEXT STEPS:

_____

_____

_____

_____

_____

_____

_____

_____

_____

• • •

On a page or two, the process may look like the above. This is all you will usually need, and you will use a verbal delivery most of the time. The headings also are not necessarily spoken (as you have seen) and will see again (Chapter 10). Having a good dialogue about a business topic is the real objective. The TPS process is the tactic to accomplish the objective (Chapter 8). In so doing you will quickly get to the point; a focused delivery commands attention and, ultimately, respect. An iterative, practiced process is the key if you are to attain the desired outcome, which is you as a "go-to" business contributor!

Of course your thought process will far exceed the finished product, as research is needed to complete the factual situation. Everything then flows from there as the big question, idea or issue will simply follow quite naturally from the facts. Developing and setting implementation steps, metric formulation, process steps, and follow-up will require a great deal of mental acuity as well. Understand that the process is very much iterative, and it is not uncommon to be mentally working on multiple plans at once.

The Six-Step TPS Process is a system that once mastered will serve you in both personal and business situations and allow you to think adroitly, succinctly, professorially, and of course businessorally. Drill it into your mind right now that all business decisions have career consequences, so think of each one as your final chance to make a lasting contribution, secure a seat at the big table, or stand for a promotion.

Before presenting a completed version of this process, let's understand the dynamics of the elements involved in it. Try picturing a funnel filled with lots of information being poured into it. In essence, the process squeezes the information thru the funnel to deliver a cogent and streamlined finished product.

Six-Step TPS Process

STEP	DYNAMIC
THE SITUATION	Facts and nothing but facts
THE BIG QUESTION, IDEA or ISSUE(s)	Obvious due to the facts
THE PLAN	Name the idea, question or issue
HOW THE PLAN WORKS	The solution(s) spelled out
HOW WE WILL MEASURE SUCCESS	Metrics defined to gauge results
IMMEDIATE NEXT STEPS	Actions spelled out to ensure success

THE SITUATION, factually developed and presented.

This initial element in the process is critically important because in short order you must impress the audience, the client, the manager, the co-worker, the analyst, or whomever you're propositioning. This is done to secure a commitment, in most cases from the one receiving your spiel to act upon your idea.

Therefore, it is logical that one must first state the situation, and to do that you need to do your research and be very factual. Nothing but facts and no "Well, I think so" or, "just maybe" or "due to unforeseen circumstances . . ." That translates to *dead on arrival*, and your time is up. The opportunity is wasted. You have lost the audience, and your reputation hangs in the balance. The chance for a second chance in business, as in major league sports, is minimal (remember Drew Bledsoe, the QB of the New England Patriots who lost his job to Tom Brady, who took his team to a half dozen Super Bowls? No, of course you don't. I am sure you don't know who Jack Welch replaced at General Electric either; see what I mean?).

While you may have graduated at the top of your class and be as bright as all get out, the playing field is cleared for all once the spotlight is on. This is where, when armed with this process the 2.0 GPA State University graduate can outshine his competition for a shot at the brass ring known as corporate cash. It matters not that the pedigree predisposes the presenter to do very well; however, his expectation level is also very high, and consequently the pressure is on to perform. Armed with facts, your unbridled confidence commands you to think and present authoritatively, adeptly, and—most importantly—*businessorally.* So, in the beginning it is all facts and nothing but the facts, so help me Bob.

An example might look just like this:

THE SITUATION: Recent market share analysis reveals BIG BOB'S cereal position has been affected by Sugar Treats' winter blitz program as share erosion continues from last year's 2.2 point decline. Trending data reveal another half point setback as our flagship brand Cheering O's is taking the biggest plunge. BIG BOB'S shelf space in key national food store chains is also suffering as new in-store cereal diagrams mandate more private label space. In-store sales representative coverage remains at the highest level as our hiring program is having a positive impact on visitation patterns. Sunday FSI (newspaper free standing coupon inserts)

penetration is at all-time low as the recent marketing shift to more broadcast media has been met with a competitive uptick in all three major supplements in the two largest newspapers. Coupon redemption remains low at 1.6 percent vs. our normal 2.3 percent in the most recent quarter.

Hopefully your continuous improvement principles are igniting, and you are pondering a few things. Paramount among them should be "why did he start there—talking about BIG BOB'S and its cereal division?" By now, after reading and beginning to implement the learnings from the first few chapters you know what matters, and you inquisitively are wondering why I am not practicing what I preach.

To begin thinking in this new way, there is a primary component that one needs to understand and implement. This one focal element sets up the thinking process seamlessly and in fact, without it you run the risk of having your thought process and eventual audience drift off into all kinds of stuff, none of which are good. The trick is to have your left-sided brain and ultimate audience in synch, as in most business situations today with all the electronic stimulants permeating the subconscious, the opportunity to be focused is minimized. Simply put, to elicit a true conversation with yourself and your eventual audience, a concerted focus is mandatory. The surefire way to accomplish it is to set parameters up front and with authority to have impact and effect all in one brief statement. Think of it as *setting the stage*. Think of it like the umpires and opposing managers going over the ground rules prior to the start of a baseball game. Think of it like the grammar school teacher saying something like—"Now class we are going to talk about geography." In so doing—creating the "frame of reference"—your brain and eventual audience clicks in to exactly what is about to be thought out and discussed and nothing more. The stage is in fact set, and it is time for the opening curtain to rise!

Yes, "focus," that simple five-letter word meaning to narrow down things, single-mindedness, or core element. In other words, at the very beginning we need to center the thought process and eventual discussion or presentation or conversation with a *frame of reference* to establish boundaries, thus preventing drifting off to other things, to exclude hidden agendas, and to ensure the purpose at hand is given its true and rightful discernment. Once established, the six steps will flow naturally as all of them relate to your established frame of reference thus creating an iterative process geared to the most desirable outcome and nothing more. And isn't it a great place to be!

Restructured with this in mind, the thinking process now looks like this:

FRAME OF REFERENCE

- THE SITUATION
- THE BIG QUESTION, BIG IDEA or BIG ISSUE(s)
- THE PLAN
- HOW THE PLAN WORKS
- HOW WE WILL MEASURE SUCCESS
- IMMEDIATE NEXT STEPS

Here is an example:

FRAME OF REFERENCE: BIG BOB'S Cereal Company— Raleigh, NC, Q4 20XX

Be very specific and be sure to seek agreement. Here you have established boundaries (the immediate paradigm) about what is to follow so you and your listeners stay within the parameters; it also aids the brain/audience in following you. The real good thing is it limits the presentation and always allows you to repudiate a particular curve ball question professionally like this: "That is out of scope for this particular meeting, but I will be glad to put this kind of analysis to work on it for you." The frame is just that, a frame like a picture frame that surrounds a picture so that your eye does not stray from the picture. It is there to grab your attention and will last as long as you are interesting and that job is largely achieved by following the next six steps.

Now reread the thinking process with the frame established to see the cohesive, aligned linkage with a narrow focus geared toward eliciting further invitation of thought and ultimate conversation about just one thing.

FRAME OF REFERENCE: BIG BOB'S Cereal Company— Raleigh, NC, Q4 20XX

THE SITUATION: Recent market share analysis reveals BIG BOB'S Q4 20XX cereal position has been affected by Sugary Treats' winter blitz program as share erosion continues from last year's 2.2 point decline. Trending data reveal another half point setback as our flagship brand Cheering O's is taking the biggest plunge. BIG BOB'S space in key national food store chains is also suffering as new in-store

cereal diagrams mandate more private label space. In-store sales representative coverage remains at the highest level as our hiring program is having a positive impact on visitation patterns. Sunday FSI (newspaper free standing coupon inserts) penetration is at all-time low as the recent marketing shift to more broadcast media has been met with a competitive uptick in all three major supplements in the two largest newspapers. Coupon redemption remains low at 1.6 percent vs. our normal 2.3 percent in the most recent quarter.

To further amplify how to think about the situation relative to the frame of reference note the learning points below:

In the situation, spell out the critical factors that drive growth or what it is you are talking about, that is, exactly what the frame of reference is. In this example I have spoken to three or four relative to Raleigh, North Carolina in Q4 20XX only—market share, shelf space, marketing, that is, advertising, and sales force penetration. There could be more so think about what is relevant and provide salient facts. Bullet points often do the trick. You will have all the backup data with you if you need it. Here you pack this with only facts like market share (remember the frame of reference and stay close to it so quoting from years ago would have little merit), recent trends, competitive thrusts, program initiative results, and so on. In other words it is the lay of the land as it answers, tell me what's going on—what's happening or "how goes it" relative to the frame of reference. Factually state it right here.

Hopefully you can see by now that the entire six steps could be a one-pager or a tome. In fact, it is either the outline or the leave-behind as you can add charts, diagrams, market share reports, personnel rankings, profit reports, competitive analysis, SWOT charts (strengths, weaknesses, opportunities, and threats), and so on. A ten page example appears in the appendix of this book.

Continuing on, the next step is:

THE BIG QUESTION: How do we leverage our larger sales force to complement the marketing initiative to reverse the negative sales trend prior to major account reviews in Q1 to affect 20XX store reset efforts?

In this case, the analysis leads to a question. It could be an *issue* or an *idea*, and in any event it is cogently obvious due to the facts.

The question or idea should fall out naturally, the audience saying to themselves, "Why didn't I think of that?" In this scenario the question might be like I have it listed here or the big idea could be the way to go but it should connect with the frame of reference or you have lost them. Selling, at its core, is a process of get 'em sick . . . get 'em well. This big question(s) is the get 'em sick part and thereafter comes the get 'em better part in "The Plan." It is important to understand that you are not necessarily looking for problems; however a factual analysis will bring them out, and if not, there is always a better way to do things, so let the analysis take you wherever it leads you. Perhaps the result is a big idea or a big issue.

Continuing on, the next step is:

THE PLAN: BIG BOB's DASH FOR CASH

With deference to the analysis name the idea, the question or the issue. This now becomes another "frame of reference." It is the definitive plan to address this particular subject. At this juncture you are half way down the funnel as skillful focusing on the get 'em well part commands amplified attention.

The plan is just a name, it doesn't have to rhyme, it could be a company sponsored program, and this is your spin on it. Usually it is your idea and a way of tracking it or think of it as your mantra.

Continuing on, the next step is:

HOW THE PLAN WORKS:

1. Starting in Q1, the Raleigh team will redeploy sales coverage according to the following:

Segment/ Share of Market	2 visits Per Week	1 visit Per Week	2 visits Per Month	2 visits Per Quarter
Grocery 46%	X			
Supercenters 17%	X			
Convenience 15%		X		
Clubs 9%			X	
Drug 5%			X	
Mass Merch 4%				X
Dollar 3%				X

This new call activity will shift focus to the top performing stores at the risk of lower volume store poaching from competitors. Bimonthly progress checks are in place to gauge competitive responses.

2. New sales member mentor program initiated that includes top performers working with all sales reps with less than one year experience.

3. Price matching in all accounts based on competitive actions.

4. Funding shifts on the fly to ensure opportunities are capitalized on.

5. A Raleigh sales force incentive contest highlighted by HQ visits and attendance at results dinner. Prizes awarded for biggest display, increased sales and display penetration.

The solution(s) are spelled out while addressing all the situational facts needing attention. Think action plans or tenets. Here you can use a paragraph to spell it out or a word chart to organize the who's, what's, and where's. In any event tell how you will capitalize on the opportunity and fix something or expand your dominance, etc. Maybe it is three or four parts and lists exactly all the steps and spells it out. The process now is three-quarters of the way down the information funnel.

Continuing on, the next step is:

HOW WE WILL MEASURE SUCCESS

MEASURE	Now	Mid-Year	Year end	+/-	Notes:
Market Share	31%	35%	38%	+7 pts	
Shelf Space	22%	25%	30%	+8 pts	
In-Store Penetration	86%	90%	96%	+10 pts	
Coupon Penetration	58%	75%	90%	+32 pts	
Coupon Redemption	1.6%	1.9%	3.1%	+1.5 pts	
Sales	100%	+ 2%	+2.4%	+2.4 pts	

These metrics are defined to gauge the results of the initiative. This part must relate exactly to the plan while linking to the situation that depicts a problem or an idea to capitalize on. I like a chart to spell it all out. Seize upon the occasion to show creativity in how you look at things but be sure to align it with company, regional, and or stretch objectives.

Continuing on, the final step is:

IMMEDIATE NEXT STEPS:

WHO	WHAT	WHEN	NOTES:
Bob	Secure funding	By Q1	
Team	Set call patterns	February	
Managers	Sell Program	March	
Finance	Establish Budgets	March	
Bob	Brand Management Buy-In	January	

Spell out the necessary actions to ensure success will be yours. Include subordinates, superiors, and everyone you need. This adds accountability and gives your team members a chance to step up. The funnel has been emptied, and now it needs to be re-loaded with another challenge. Go for it.

Here is this exact Six Step Process TPS Process:

FRAME OF REFERENCE: BIG BOB'S Cereal Company— Raleigh, NC, Q4 20XX

THE SITUATION: Recent market share analysis reveals BIG BOB'S cereal position has been affected by Sugary Treats' winter blitz program as share erosion continues from last year's 2.2 point decline. Trending data reveal another half point setback as our flagship brand Cheering O's is taking the biggest plunge. BIG BOB'S space in key national food store chains is also suffering as new in-store cereal diagrams mandate more private label space. In-store sales representative coverage remains at the highest level as our hiring program is having a positive impact on visitation patterns. Sunday FSI penetration (newspaper free standing coupon inserts) is at an all-time low as the recent marketing shift to more broadcast media has been met with a competitive uptick in all three major supplements in the two largest newspapers. Coupon redemption remains low at 1.6 percent vs. our normal 2.3 percent in the most recent quarter.

THE BIG QUESTION: How do we leverage our larger sales force to complement the marketing initiative to reverse the negative sales trend prior to major account reviews to affect up-coming store reset efforts?

THE PLAN: BIG BOB's DASH FOR CASH

HOW THE PLAN WORKS:

1. Starting in Q1, the Raleigh team will re-deploy sales coverage according to the following:

Segment/Share of Market	2 visits Per Week	1 visit Per Week	2 visits Per Month	2 visits Per Quarter
Grocery 46%	X			
Supercenters 17%	X			
Convenience 15%		X		
Clubs 9%			X	

Drug 5%			X	
Mass Merch 4%				X
Dollar 3%				X

This new call activity will shift focus to the top performing stores at the risk of lower volume store poaching from competitors. Bimonthly progress checks are in place to gauge competitive responses.

2. New sales member mentor program initiated that includes top performers working with all sales reps with less than one year experience.

3. Price matching in all accounts based on competitive actions.

4. Funding shifts on the fly to ensure opportunities are capitalized on.

5. A Raleigh sales force incentive contest highlighted by HQ visits and attendance at results dinner. Prizes awarded for biggest display, increased sales and display penetration.

HOW WE WILL MEASURE SUCCESS:

MEASURE	Now	Mid-Year	Year end	+/-	Notes:
Market Share	31%	35%	38%	+7 pts	
Shelf Space	22%	25%	30%	+8 pts	
In-Store Penetration	86%	90%	96%	+10 pts	
Coupon Penetration	58%	75%	90%	+32 pts	
Coupon Redemption	1.6%	1.9%	3.1%	+1.5 pts	
Sales	100%	+ 2%	+2.4%	+2.4 pts	

IMMEDIATE NEXT STEPS:

WHO	WHAT	WHEN	NOTES:
Bob	Secure funding	By Q1	
Team	Set call patterns	February	
Managers	Sell Program	March	
Finance	Establish Budgets	March	
Bob	Brand Management Buy-In	January	

• • •

How does this fit in the larger scope of the business world? Actually, it fits in perfectly because you now have a process that relates to thinking about, presenting, and selling yourself and your plan in the real business world. This logical flow of information elicits active listening. To that end, I believe listening is more important than speaking, for when one listens he has the opportunity to learn. When one speaks he has the conspicuous excuse to bloviate. The balance ought to be about 70–30 percent toward listening if you are truly to be heard and revered as opposed to just being loud.

Subscribing to this process will allow you to focus on your developmental thoughts. Subsequently, the concentrated delivery will permit your audience to actively listen to you as well. Being succinct, targeted, and logical are antidotes for presentation failure. Thus, the TPS Process is failure resistant. TPS, when mastered is alluring, even captivating, and establishes you as an informed, intelligent and integral team member. It is good to have impact. It is good to be valued. It is good to be effective. Master this process.

By the way, how about the up and coming business guy in the New York City elevator . . . remember him? Might I have catapulted myself a few notches up the corporate ladder if only I articulated a plan in that impromptu elevator meeting with the big guy? Keep that vivid picture in your mind, as your elevator ride is just around the corner.

So, why didn't I or why wasn't I able to articulate a plan in that elevator? Part of the answer lies in the fact that in addition to not knowing how to cohesively think and write or deliver a compelling plan, I also had not yet acquired the understanding of what it means to be successful, and just as importantly, that success is all about being competent. These two things—understanding success (Chapter 6) and being competent (Chapter 7) are what matter, and they were being learned along the way. Business planning was in the blood—Pop was letting me gain some experience—the hard way!

I do submit that by staying in the inquiry mode, understanding indispensable concepts, and successfully thinking through critical decisions, you will understand what really matters in your business life. Subsequently, you will be in a far better place to make critical decisions. In the game of business, failure can never be an option, and neither should not thinking. Thomas Edison proclaimed that only a small percentage of us think. Peculiarly attempting to go one step further, how about this: Think—even when it hurts! And take solace in the knowledge that you can think your way through to a successful and rewarding business career.

This chapter addresses the essence of the book, the things you don't necessarily learn in college but serve you well the rest of your business life. Reread this chapter and practice using the

TPS concept routinely and for every aspect of your business. You should have a plan for every initiative in addition to a master plan.

$$\bullet \ \bullet \ \bullet$$

To my father, Pop, the top three business decisions he made centered on what would drive customers to his business, that is, how to promote the business (himself), what will keep customers coming back, and how to stay ahead of the competition.

So, my fatherly advice:

- Take your three personal improvement areas and write a plan for each of them!

- Take your three familial improvement areas and write a plan for each of them!

- Take your top three personal business improvement areas and write a plan for each of them!

- Prepare your sixty-second elevator pitch now: How is your business?

- Have a business plan in your pocket at all times.

- Check out the appendix of this book for a 10-page TPS review with the frame of reference being, "Writing a Non-Fiction Business Book." It is the narrative about how this very book came to be.

Let's converse about focused energy, being competent, and being successful; and understanding the concept of "trial and triumph" while using the art of conversation to attain lofty goals in your business life.

5

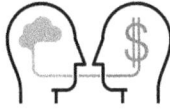

Working Thankfully

"Work is nothing more than energy focused on a task"

Bob Pettinelli

Born of immigrant parents and raised in the Great Depression era, Pop had the innate capacity to be happy simply to have work to do, just like his father. It was my grandfather, the man whose birthday I was born on, who instilled a great work ethic in his American family. His routine was to focus on one thing at a time and concentrate all his energy on doing whatever he was doing to the fullest. Let's talk about energy focused on a task.

WORK. That thing most everyone does routinely, yet without work our routine becomes just plain mundane. What is work? Is it really important? Why do we do it? Can we do without it?

Why do so many people truly despise working? Why is everyone in such a hurry to reach retirement? Do they hate being held accountable or being told what to do? Is there a natural disdain or latent agenda against leadership, management, or authority of any kind? Is work too shackling for some, or maybe even for many? Is work so egregious to one's makeup that the mere thought of it spins folks into a state of malaise? Perhaps there is a perverse sense of "I can do it better than the boss; I can make a go of life without it." Or maybe there is just a lack of motivation in one's character to go out and make the world—your world—a better place.

The answer to some of those ruminations might be yes, but given that most of us manage to make a go of it, I would say, "Hell no!" Work is indispensable if you are to make life interesting, manageable, and—dare I say—enjoyable. Put another way, without work, life is without energy; without work life follows a path without predefined destinations; without work life is unfocused, even meaningless; without work, life is almost not living.

The trick or essence of work is to boil it down to a series of tasks bounded by a well-defined plan. No, you don't need to possess an extremely detailed set of plans, like those for a 15,000 square foot mansion. Thankfully, life is not that difficult. Anywhere between a cogent thought to a master written plan will do, but be sure to actually *think* about a plan, for in life and as in business, it really matters that the wind is always at your back.

Plan your work, work your plan. It is probably one of the simplest yet most powerful messages anyone can receive, understand, and act upon. Heck, it's right up there with the concept of supply and demand. Better yet, it falls nicely into what I believe work is all about, a series of life's tasks.

Working

Work parallels planning. The two are intricately intermingled such that planning without execution is an exercise in futility. Be diligent and plan your work, plan your future, plan your life, plan to be successful, and above all plan for the unexpected. Put another way—if you fail to plan, you may as well plan to fail. Have a goal; have a plan. Work toward the goal (Chapter 8). Planning your work and working your plan coupled with knowing know how to think in six concurrent steps (Chapter 4) makes planning your work a much simpler task. Don't over-complicate this. Work is simply energy focused on a task. The main point is to plan your work to know what you are going to do rather than finding out what you did!

Never forget, however, that work should not be the end all of one's existence. Rather, working is a means to an end. The reason to work is to enjoy and challenge yourself so that you can feel good about yourself and your ability to tackle life's challenges. It is how you choose to tackle the challenges that will be the true measure of your existence and not how many material things you collect along the way.

To fully understand the broader overall concept of work, suppose everyone worked on a commission basis, like a real estate agent, a commissioned salesperson, or any self-employed person who must generate their own paycheck. How about a mother or father and the clergy? If everyone had to demonstrate their value on a daily basis, mankind would be settling on planets far beyond Mars as the continuous improvement spirit would speed up the process to unfathomable velocities. Most successful people work like they are on a true commission arrangement regardless their compensation plan. A wise approach to working is to feel and work like you are paying yourself; just allow someone else to compensate you.

Where should the energy be placed is the real continuous improvement thought. The fact that you are accomplished at mastering complex documents like building schematics, stock market gyrations, or quantum physics is not what's really important. Rather, expending energy (working) via focusing on one thing at a time and in due time will serve you well if you have mastered the concepts of critical thinking and continuous improvement. These concepts will become truly invaluable in your life. They will prepare you for the inevitable curveballs that life will throw at you, thus preventing them from ensuring that your journey through life is largely downhill.

• • •

OK, Bob, so how does this all work in the larger scope of the business world? Working, or the ability to work, is the sole conduit for your business success. Just like the goal of any business venture is to secure a sustainable competitive advantage, your goal is to secure a roof over your head and put food on the table for yourself and your family. It is called survival, which is pretty basic stuff. Anything above that is gravy. Your competitive advantage is the ability to work and to do that you need to focus your energy on tasks. The question becomes what are the indispensable, quintessential, and very personal business tasks you need to focus on?

The specific answer will differ for each of us, but in general they are threefold. Just like my father and grandfather before me, focus adroitly on these three things that ultimately matter:

1. Master Something

Your skill set must be admired by others so that you will be rewarded financially for working. The skills must always be relevant and therefore transferable. It is the exact opposite of resting on your laurels. Delete that idea from your mind.

I'm not talking about acquiring an advanced degree necessarily, but you must possess a personal and sustainable indispensable competency or two. You can gain insight via a personal SWOT analysis (strengths, weaknesses, opportunities, and threats). Properly executed, the personal SWOT will show you what you can leverage from the foundational building blocks of your strengths and opportunities. The weaknesses and threats side of the ledger will also reveal current and potential roadblocks you must overcome as you work toward a personal sustainable core competency. Using the aforementioned Six-Step TPS process against this task is a natural starting point.

Endeavor to create a personal sustainable competitive advantage like the windows operating system is to Microsoft or the value Steve Jobs was to Apple. As legendary CEO Jack Welch proclaimed, "If you don't have a competitive advantage, don't compete." You must master something, as it is never quite good enough to be good at a lot of things while mastering none. The key is not to be better than anyone and everyone; it is to be better tomorrow. Keep grinding with a purpose.

2. *Be Principled*

Have a purpose in everything you do. Establishing a set of principles to guide you provides that purpose. Think of principles as the ground wire in an electrical socket. Grounding principles create a safety net to prevent electrical fires. In life and business, this allows you to reach higher and farther because of this perpetual safety net. At a minimum these grounding principles should address and stress ethics, team orientation, integrity, and loyalty.

Working ethically allows you to go about your business with a smile knowing full well that your main goal is the best interests of everyone concerned. A "team first" posture serves everyone. Moreover, by exhibiting such behaviors, leadership manifests itself in your principles without the mention of the "I" word. The idea is to exude principles with nary a mention of them. Walk around with them; enact them in everything you do. Adopt a posture of communicate, navigate, and illuminate by always being principled. In fact, an acquaintance of mine, Ed Sprague, so abhors the "I" word that he prefaces his entertaining and informative book *The Z Factor* by "explanin'" how *I*, *Me*, and *My* rub people the wrong way. I concur wholeheartedly. The word "I" is among the shortest in the English language, and I believe it should be the least used word in your business lexicon.

Lastly, loyalty should always be ceded to the organization and not necessarily to any individual.

The person is here today and gone tomorrow while the organization remains. Being loyal to the greater good is the principal lesson to follow.

Being grounded in ethics with a team first posture, all the while exhibiting integrity and loyalty (and other principles) allows you to work unselfishly and relentlessly on projects that matter. Subscribing to the greater good philosophy is the hallmark quality of a successful person and—dare I say—a leader.

Always surround yourself with principled people. If you ever wonder why the guy equal to you got promoted over you—now you know why. Being principled is the intangible tie breaker. These organic traits are hard to teach and even harder to cultivate, but every leader looks for them and will surround himself with focused, energetic, and principled people. Be one of them, just like my youngest son Mike, who has received among other accolades an award for professionalism and ethics. He is grounded. He is principled. He is focused. While in his twenties he was vice-president for a global leader in insurance broking and risk management consulting. By the age of thirty, Mike managed worldwide insurance and risk management for a major international company.

3. *Focus on Focusing*

Focusing is an art. Distractions abound, and in corporate life expect to be pulled and prodded in every direction. The toughest part of living in a corporate world is managing people above you.

Leading yourself and your team is uncomplicated compared to managing the impulses of the anointed overseers. Your supervisor, you, and your subordinates is a trifecta wrought with peril. Shifting winds are the norm in corporate life but *you* must provide the calm with your team and provide positive spin to the latest whim. No matter your position, you will have to continually adjust, accepting that management has more and better information than you do to implement a 180-degree change in direction. Or, as the legendary martial arts expert Bruce Lee once stated, "The successful warrior is the average man, with laser-like focus."

Learn how to focus and as an exemplar having a business plan in your pocket at all times is exactly what focusing is all about.

Never forget the basics: work is energy focused on a task. Not mundane, yet magical. Not routine, yet required. And certainly not drudgery but almost drug-like in that it provides the so wonderfully hallucinogenic effect of sustaining your whole being and it isn't even sinful. Work is to be treasured and respected. Work is delightfully time consuming and emotionally draining, and when you think about it, work is really the essence of living. Learn to love working!

Work is a series of endless tasks. Knowing where to focus your energies allows you to conquer every challenge. The whole process of work won't be so daunting if you focus on principles while you develop your personal and sustainable core competencies. Learn from winners like Jack Welch who stated in his book *Winning* "People with positive energy are generally extroverted and optimistic. They start the day with enthusiasm and usually end it that way too, rarely seeming to tire in the middle. They don't complain about working hard; they love to work."

• • •

To my father, Pop, the top three things he continually worked on centered on working smarter, outworking the competition, and working collaboratively with staff, vendors, and customers to ensure he sustained his competitive advantage.

So, my fatherly advice:

- Take your top three personal business improvement areas and augment them to master one or more skills. Add a personal SWOT analysis to the game plan. This is called working smarter. Don't envy those who possesses a sustainable core competency. Be that person!

- Ground yourself in principles. Communicate, navigate, and illuminate with a principled posture. Know exactly what you stand for. Look to your mentors and admired business leaders for inspiration and emulate them. Champion your own principles.

- Focus, focus, focus on things that matter. You will expend positive energy while focusing on tasks that really matter. Re-read Chapter 2, on "What Matters: *Simply Stated.*" Cultivate perspective and apply a laser-like focus to stay on track.

- "Whistle while you work." Be thankful and be in the game. Practice the guidelines in this book, and you will always be engaged, always learning, and always improving yourself.

- Rewrite and tighten up your sixty-second elevator pitch: how is *your* business now?

Let's delve into the exciting possibilities of being competent and being successful; and understanding the concept of "trial and triumph" while using the art of conversation to attain lofty goals in your business life.

6

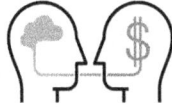

Success
Perpetually

"If you don't design your own life plan,
chances are you'll fall into someone else's plan.
And guess what they have planned for you? Not much."

Jim Rohn

Pop's makeup was such that success was the unspoken goal. He didn't talk much about it—he just acted that way. He didn't have much time to plan for success either. He was too busy being successful. How did he do it? Let's talk about being perpetually successful.

SUCCESS. So much has been said, discussed, pontificated upon, and written about how to have success. Sure, there are many "how to" books about success but from what context? Usually it is how to be successful at picking stocks, investing in real estate, planning your retirement, valuing currency, or even mastering quantum economics. But what about long lasting business success? Well, that's why you picked up this particular book.

I might not have the conclusive "Keys to Individual Success," but if you put together all of the elements of this book you will at the very least have the bedrock from which to build the pillars of your success. By understanding and practicing these concepts you will be positioning yourself for foundational growth, ultimately leading to eventual and perpetual success. One (eventual) without the other (perpetual) falls woefully short in the quest for true, sustainable success, for without sustainability success is fleeting; without sustainability success is hollow; without sustainability success is really just another label.

Success is not finite; it evolves, and it is always too late to be celebrated, for it is always behind you—the minute you reach it, you cannot feel it anymore. I liken success to the very essence of business as in its quest for a truly *sustainable competitive advantage* (SCA), the business entity constantly strives to either build the SCA or maintain, if not grow, its stature to broaden the competitive gap between itself and its competitors. Corny photos adorning corner offices don't define success. Rather, success involves working only on what really matters; it's about saying "yes" to continuous improvement principles. Once you understand that "what really matters" is the essence of success, you then only need to master its tenets to be routinely and repeatedly successful. Granted, that's a big "only," but nobody ever said success was going to be easy.

One thing is for sure: you will never get anywhere without a well-tuned "inner compass" that not only always guides you in the right direction, it complements your knowledge, pedigree, and experience that others can't quite pinpoint but are certain that you have (and they wish they did). Respectful adulation and not necessarily recognition may be your primary reward. But if you turn around and someone is following you, then you are like the master (leader) is to a puppy (follower). You have what they want, and it translates to leadership—masterfully, skillfully, almost scientifically being continuously successful.

There are a million quotes for success, but here is my two cents worth: the essence of success is really the "how to" or action plan undergirding it; the journey defines it. The principles underlying success provide the true excitement. Perspective and redemption only come from building up your success. You stop worrying about failure when you instinctively know that you have the skill and knowledge that always creates a blueprint for success regardless of the challenge.

• • •

Well, Bob, you might ask, how does all this matter in the larger scope of the business world? Honestly, it only matters if you dare to be successful. It only matters if you want to provide more than a roof over your head and food on the table for yourself and your family. It only matters if you want to challenge yourself to play on the big field. And it only matters if you want your children to go further than you have!

What follows are the keys to individual success:

1. DEVELOP A CORE COMPETENCY

2. UNDERSTAND YOUR STRENGTHS and WEAKNESSES

3. BE AGGRESSIVE WHEN IT COMES YOUR CAREER

4. HAVE A PLAN

5. ADOPT A PURPOSEFUL POSTURE

6. PORTRAY A POSITIVE OUTLOOK

7. SELECT THE INDIVIDUALS YOU WORK WITH CAREFULLY

8. DEMONSTRATE THAT YOU ARE A TEAM PLAYER

9. DON'T BE AFRAID TO SAY NO

10. ACCEPT THAT MONEY IS NOT ALWAYS THE MOST IMPORTANT ASPECT OF YOUR CAREER

11. OVERCOMMUNICATE

12. THINK

In line with the continuous improvement style the keys are presented with contemplations or checkpoints to evaluate and grow your position. Check yourself against these twelve traits as you read them. Anything less than an eleven means you have work to do. Anything nearing a one means you have a lot of work to do and that's OK, now that you understand what work is. After all, you can't achieve success until you fully understand it. The previous chapters lend themselves to assisting you in the attainment of goals. Is possessing perpetual success traits a goal of yours? Don't you think it should be?

• • •

Keys to Individual Success

DEVELOP A CORE COMPETENCY
Make sure it is transferable!

To even be minimally successful, there is no substitute for a foundational core competency. It is mandatory for every field of business, with no exceptions. It's also crucial for this competency to be transferable. Staying with the same company (or probably even the same career) for thirty or forty years just does not happen anymore. The flexibility of easily transferable competencies is better than gold when it comes to your long-term viability in the world of business. Today's career paths more often than not resemble a twisted maze filled with potholes, curvy roads, and forked turns. When you possess transferable skills, it straightens out the road and creates the wind at your back that is so vital to keep moving forward.

Checkpoints:

- What is a core competency that plays an important role in your work and how do you develop and maintain one in order to be successful?
- Is more than one core competency needed to be successful?
- Why is transferring a competency so critical? If someone's current situation is working well, isn't that good enough? (Hint: turn around and no one is following you yet. Remember, your goal is perpetual success; consider anything less than that a failure.)

Continued ...

DEVELOP A CORE COMPETENCY
Make sure it is transferable!

Takeaway:

Skills, aptitudes, proficiencies—call them what you will, but it's absolutely imperative to have at least one, maybe two that are transferable—the more the merrier. Look at the successful people around you and figure out how they got there. Begin by emulating them and quicken the pace. Jump into the race and be determined to win it. If you do things right, before long others will start copying your ways.

Big Questions, Ideas, or Issues:

- Minimally or wildly successful? Which aspiration truly defines you?
- Identify impediments and rid yourself of them now. Today (i.e., not tomorrow!) is a good day to start this process. Make it a personal obligation. If it suits your personality, get mad about it. Do whatever it takes to eliminate the obstacles.
- Think strategically in this endeavor, never forgetting that it is foundational to individual and perpetual success.

UNDERSTAND YOUR STRENGTHS
and WEAKNESSES
Know Thyself

Know your weakness and opportunities, too. A finely tuned personal SWOT analysis will allow for true introspection unlike anything else. It's a starting point in your quest to find your inner strength. Once you understand those, you can grow from there to whatever heights you can imagine. Liftoff!

Checkpoints:

- Do you know your strengths and weaknesses and is that enough to know? Have you embraced a 360-degree peer feedback session— direct feedback from peers, subordinates, and supervisors compared to your self-evaluation? Feedback is used to plan and map specific development paths.
- What opportunities do you have to grow? Who/ what is blocking your way?
- Is a personal SWOT analysis enough to really know yourself?

Continued ...

UNDERSTAND YOUR STRENGTHS
and WEAKNESSES
Know Thyself

Takeaway:

A heartfelt SWOT analysis is a good beginning for self-understanding. Add in a 360-degree peer feedback session, which is equally valuable. Coupled together these two liberators provide insightful perspective and soulful redemption. Dig deep inside to find out who you are and who you will be. You may even surprise yourself once you get in there and find out what really makes you tick.

Big Questions, Ideas, or Issues:

- Reflect but don't overanalyze yourself. It can constrain your creativity.
- Dwell on your positive attributes; cultivate new ones currently lacking in your personal repertoire. Build them into a treasure trove of lasting principles. Embrace feedback. Use fear as a motivator.
- Can you imagine yourself running a company? Why or why not? And of course, just what exactly does that look like?

BE AGGRESSIVE
WHEN IT COMES TO YOUR CAREER
Period.

There are times to be aggressive and times to back off. Aggressive driving is never good. Acquiescing to defensive driving is very good. When it comes to managing your career you need to be extremely aggressive. Assert yourself; create some whiplash. It's mother's milk!

Checkpoints:

- Whose career is it?
- Whose career is it?
- Whose career is it?

Continued ...

BE AGGRESSIVE
WHEN IT COMES TO YOUR CAREER
Period.

Takeaway:

Recognize the only stop sign in your career is potentially you because it is after all your career. There is no rear view mirror—don't look back. The traffic signal is always green, and you never have to worry about a speeding ticket. There are in fact no speed limits—go as fast as you want to. Aggressively drive your career in the fast lane like it's the Indy 500. Godspeed!

Big Questions, Ideas, or Issues:

- Be the green light in your career. Turn it on. Turn it up. Put the pedal to the metal and peel out!
- Mario Andretti aggressively set out to be the greatest race car driver of all time. He not only won at Indy and Daytona and everywhere else he raced, he ended up being named (better yet, he earned the title) driver of the century! Imagine if he had meekly settled for putting around in a go-cart to kill a Saturday afternoon?
- When it comes to your career, the choice is yours: a go-cart or a Formula One race car? Punch it, full speed ahead with no looking back. Win the checkered flag. Drink from the milk bottle!

HAVE A PLAN
Revisit It Frequently

Have a plan; have an idea. When you plan out your career you will stimulate your creativity. You will sharpen your strategic thinking capabilities. You will become more factual and more precise. Problems will be solved innovatively and effectively. Ambiguity will be neutralized. Good plans enhance the competitive advantage. They enrich operational economies. They encourage innovation.

Checkpoints:

- Do you have a life plan?
- Do you have a business plan?
- What are your contingency plans?

Continued ...

HAVE A PLAN
Revisit It Frequently

Takeaway:

If being more creative and thus a better strategic thinker is the result of planning then sign up for an advanced class. Acquiring or enhancing these two qualities alone are sufficient reason to quickly set out on a course to address your future. Uncertainty is useless; uniqueness is unbounded. Have a unique plan? Precisely.

Big Questions, Ideas, or Issues:

- My life plan centers on . . .
- My business plan includes . . .
- When I reach my goals I will feel like . . .
- Planning without execution is merely an exercise in futility. Even worse, it's a complete waste of time.

ADOPT A PURPOSEFUL POSTURE
Stay Focused

Drive, determination, dedication—all worthy attributes defining a winning posture. All require immense focus. All need to be the adopted philosophy. Why? Because, if not lassitude, lethargy and laziness become you. Make a goal. Focus on it. Make it actionable. Do it on purpose. Be in the game to win it. Settle for nothing less than MVP—Most Valuable Player—and absolutely never just stand there watching the action unfold like a spectator.

Checkpoints:

- Are you driven by goals? Are you determined to exceed your goals? Have you exceeded any goals? If so, how long ago? Fear indifference; it's idiotic.
- Do you proclaim to be driven by a purpose in life; in business? To whom do you propose such endeavors? Sharing is redemptive.
- Focus on focusing. It makes choices easier. Focus on your purpose. Adopt the Army motto: Be all that you can be! Join your own army. Be the general. Win.

Continued ...

ADOPT A PURPOSEFUL POSTURE
Stay Focused

Takeaway:

Act, not react. Reaction is not the opposite of action. Reaction is not redemption. Philosophy aside, indifference is juxtaposed to purposeful posture. Why be daft when you can be dogged? This is an effortless choice. Embrace being dogged. It's new and it's you. Focusing is resistant to fear. It chases it away like light does a shadow.

Big Questions, Ideas, or Issues:

- What have you done on purpose lately?
- Can you or should you dedicate your purposeful posture to your father? He can guide you. When is the last time you two had a meaningful conversation? Dare to be dogged!

PORTRAY A POSITIVE OUTLOOK
No Matter the Situation

When you think about it, there really is no other choice. In fact, the opposite outlook is one of the Top Five reasons for limiting a career. Negative people see problems; positive people see results. Think about the people you know in your own life from both categories, and you will immediately realize just how true this is. Envision success. Be euphoric about new opportunities. Disregard skepticism; welcome challenges. Drama lives in Hollywood; leave it there. Smile.

Checkpoints:

- Remember that it take less muscle power to smile than frown.
- Who wants to hang around with a downer?
- Can you capture good-time feelings on demand?

Continued ...

PORTRAY A POSITIVE OUTLOOK
No Matter the Situation

Takeaway:

Never thought about the opposite of a successful career? Negativity is a top career stopper. It is quite depressing, actually, because it's all about how you can fail rather than being about how you can succeed (Chapter 9). If your career is important to you, I'm not saying to wear rose-colored glasses. I am saying to accept the reality. Check your emotions at the door; it's a job, not an acting class. Rebuild and rebrand if you have to. Select your work environment carefully. Resist the nay-sayers. They are invariably the losers who always fail. As for you: aim high!

Big Questions, Ideas, or Issues:

- Attitude equals altitude.
- Work like you are self-employed; just allow someone else to pay you.
- Stay positive and explore career starters for yourself. Can you name some? Have you read about any lately? Perhaps today? If not, why not? (And when do the excuses end?)

SELECT THE INDIVIDUALS YOU WORK WITH
Carefully

Work—love it. People—eh, sometimes. What gives? Maybe it's the competition for advancement or just poor sandbox skills. Good work environments are enjoyable and exhilarating. Judiciously select your team. Contribute to it, nurture it, expand, and enhance it, or change it. Nothing can turn an enjoyable career into a slice of hell faster than insufferable colleagues. I'm not saying up and quit at the first sign of irritation (a certain amount of it is inevitable and unavoidable). You do, however, need to be very discriminating in the choices you make in this area. Otherwise, this is something that could really hold you back for years to come. Choose wisely.

Checkpoints:

- Ask yourself these three questions as if you owned an upstart, fledgling company that was hiring employees using your money:
    - Would you spend your money to hire them?
    - On make or break projects would you work with them?
    - Someday would you work for them?
- Do your associates possess unquestioned moral character?
- Can you teach and learn from your co-workers?

Continued ...

SELECT THE INDIVIDUALS YOU WORK WITH
Carefully

Takeaway:

Accept there are all kinds of associates. Surround yourself with people possessing high morals and who enjoy your idea of work. Don't worry about being "judgmental" in this regard. This is business we're talking about here, and if you don't do whatever is necessary to further your career, rest assured that nobody else will do it for you. Help create the sandbox. Spend corporate cash like it was your own money. Teach more than you learn. Change what you can; fret not over the disenchanted.

Big Questions, Ideas, or Issues:

- If it ain't broke don't fix it; but make it better . . . always.
- Work on a tropical island or work in Manhattan. It's the same thing—think about it! One just has the sand. Bring your morals to work along with your brain. You won't get very far if you forget or neglect either.
- Upon leaving your position, is it a better place to be?

DEMONSTRATE
THAT YOU ARE A TEAM PLAYER
We vs. I

Or should it be us? Teams abound in modern business; we create something out of nothing, we build mountains, and we win battles. Me, I contribute like you do. Me and you, we are better than I. Assist, inspire, and encourage to validate your value. Show your spirit. It's all about us. Take my weakness and make it into a strength, and I will do the same for you.

Checkpoints:

- Is your loyalty to an individual or (rightfully so) to the organization?
- Do you have to, or want to, work on your current team?
- Do you sacrifice for the greater good or solely for yourself?

Continued ...

DEMONSTRATE
THAT YOU ARE A TEAM PLAYER
We vs. I

Takeaway:

The team and/or the organization is the highest form of enterprise. Enterprising individuals make up a good team, a team that you should want to work on. Being loyal to both tops loyalty to just one of them. Authentic and invigorating team players stimulate spirit. We is us; be we.

Big Questions, Ideas, or Issues:

- Have you ever climbed a mountain by yourself? If you fall, who is there to help to get back up on your feet again?
- Collaborate and corroborate whenever you can. Both actions certify your contributing posture. They heighten camaraderie. These actions raise the bar, and they also provide a grassroots form of leadership that others will readily follow.
- Whatever the endeavor, bring your friend *we*.

DON'T BE AFRAID TO SAY NO
No is Really an Upside-Down Yes

No, no thank you, or hell no—what is the difference? Tone. Impact is delivered and felt via the accompanying tone. Be it factual or emphatic, the answer is still no. There is a place for no in the business world. It's fine to politely say no when the facts say so. Negotiate alternatives; live in reality. Get to yes. Recognize that "no" is not about being negative; to the contrary, it's about providing the appropriate and accurate response for a given situation. In fact, when you look at it from that perspective, it is a positive response that is used to move the ball forward with the right decision leading to a responsible plan of action.

Checkpoints:

- Do you always make fact-based decisions?
- Can you or should you say no to your mother?
- How do you react to "no"?

Continued ...

DON'T BE AFRAID TO SAY NO
No is Really an Upside-Down Yes

Takeaway:

It's OK to say no. It just requires facts, tact, and diplomacy to do it right. The delivery is set by the tone. The emphasis speaks to the severity of the action. By negotiating solutions, such as "If I do this for you; will you do this for me?" allows for real dialogue and alternative ways to say yes. This is an acquired skill that you can constantly improve.

Big Questions, Ideas, or Issues:

- Have you ever been denied a pay raise or rejected or passed over for a promotion? If so, someone told you no. Your reaction says a lot about your character.
- A fact-based "no" is palatable. Reality calls for some "no(s)" along the way. You will be giving and receiving them; ensure the ramifications are understood. It's just another decision. Make it—accept it—move on. Dwelling on it is a huge mistake that sends you into the Land of the Whiners, a place where you never want to go.
- There is a 50/50 chance of something being yes or no. Contrary to the old song, "No" doesn't have to be *"the saddest experience you'll ever know."*

ACCEPT THAT MONEY IS NOT ALWAYS THE MOST IMPORTANT ASPECT OF YOUR CAREER
Accept and Conquer Challenges

Why accept challenges? Because without them you cannot grow. Cash can't buy courage or grit or tenacity. Focus on the challenge, not the cash, to make even more money. Accepting and conquering challenges enriches your character over time—another literally invaluable trait money cannot buy.

Checkpoints:

- If your salary was quadrupled could you produce more?
- What percentile would you be in if the world worked on commission?
- Imagine if primary school teachers were paid what orthopedic surgeons, rock stars and commercial real estate moguls were paid. Would we have better teachers, more or fewer teachers, and would the world be more advanced or less advanced because of it?

Continued ...

ACCEPT THAT MONEY IS NOT ALWAYS THE MOST IMPORTANT ASPECT OF YOUR CAREER
Accept and Conquer Challenges

Takeaway:

Personal growth must occur if one is to succeed. To grow one must reach the stretch objectives. If conquering challenges builds character, then why not try to build a skyscraper? You can't spend character but then again can you? You bet you can. It's called human capital; got any? Now, how many stories do you want for that skyscraper?

Big Questions, Ideas, or Issues:

- Is money really a motivator?
- Experience trumps cash knowing full-well the latter will come to those deserving of its just reward.
- At your core, be like a primary school teacher. There is no greater challenge to conquer. Being noble is being rich. Be both.

OVERCOMMUNICATE
Not Merely Inform

Over communicate by eliminating unnecessary frequency. Is that an oxymoron? Adopt this rule: communicate only to educate and empower and not to entertain. Only then will it have impact. Too much of it conditions people to ignore it. Be brief, be factual, and be heard. You can always say more with less. Getting there quickly is an art. There is no time for wordy explanations. The business world got to 140 characters or less before there was a Twitter. Make every word move the ball forward; just dribbling it gets you nowhere.

Checkpoints:

- There is a lot of noise; yet not enough ideas are being exchanged.
- Over communication is not open communication . . . or is it?
- When speaking, writing, or presenting are you just saying a lot of stuff or are you actually communicating?

Continued ...

OVERCOMMUNICATE
Not Merely Inform

Takeaway:

One vexing thing in the business world lies in the communication area. In general, there is just too much of it. Instead of informing to cover the pro-verbial buttocks, strive to energize. Do you really think communicating is copying the world on every memo you write? Convey ideas and solutions. Communicate results, not the method.

Big Questions, Ideas, or Issues:

- Ask or tell? Great question! Over or open? Over easy!
- Think of cc's as crummy communication.
- Communicate about the results, not the method.
- Exchange thoughts; foster growth. Scream silently.

THINK
Even When It Hurts

Thinking runs the gamut from *"think nothing of it"* to *"think twice."* Remember that Thomas Edison said most people exercise no thoughts at all. Twice thinking is taxing. You do get paid to think, be it creatively or extensively to make processes better and to maximize efforts. Thinking is mandatory, so exercise your brain daily, even when it hurts! Brain jog; not brain fog!

Checkpoints:

- You get paid to get things done. Inherently that means expediently and proficiently. The more you think, the more you can get done and with far better efficiency.
- The only problem with the human mind is that it doesn't come with instructions on how to use it. Exercise it to maximize its full potential.
- Are thoughtful actions just a 9-to-5 thing? Extracurricular? Exhausting? Do you completely forget all thoughts of business after business hours are over? Is that always a good idea?

Continued ...

THINK
Even When It Hurts

Takeaway:

Thinking is really all about mental acuity and not mental IQ. There is only one Edison. You can't exceed his brain power, can you? But you can sharpen your perspective and share insights. You can be a far-sighted, quixotic, and even quintessential contributor always. Being cerebral doesn't have to be intellectual. Be intuitive, instinctive, and insightful to be in the top 5 percent of the thinkers. It's a trifecta that never misses.

Big Questions, Ideas, or Issues:

- The enduring business question is, what do you think?
- Set out to create your own brainchild—the lightbulb is already taken. But that "lightbulb" primed and ready to go off in your head just might be the next bright idea the world is waiting to see.
- Streamline your thought process. Think adroitly not disparately.

• • •

Have you nurtured this subject anywhere else? Perhaps you have, but has it sunk in? Can you relate to this? Perhaps you can, but have you practiced being successful? Of the dozen traits how many have you cultivated? Perhaps you possess some of them; when will all of them be part of you? Can you think of more?

Having discussed business with many captains of industry I can tell you that most have mastered these traits and more. They are relentless in the application of them. They exude these traits. You would notice them almost immediately upon meeting these people. Moreover, they demand them from everyone around them. They surround themselves with people of like traits, that is, successful people possess successful traits.

But there's much more to the story. Possessing these traits is not sufficient for very successful people. Nor is displaying them and exuding them. In fact, the best of the best don't settle for less than full attainment of these characteristics. No, success is the exponential result of championing all of these traits continually and naturally. The magic to realizing perpetual success is to synthesize all of the traits into one outstanding characteristic and it is simply *urgency*. Possessing this one trait of purposeful posture is tantamount to attaining perpetual success. Yes, success equates to urgency. Tuck that into your brain and don't let go of it. Your success is urgent! Tackle the challenges without delay (in layman's terms: you snooze, you lose). You should identify all the impediments that hinder your success and find a way to squash them. Now. (A good place to start is with your personal SWOT Analysis and specifically the weaknesses and threats side of the ledger.) When success becomes your passionate desire, you will outright own it.

Successful business leaders are in the know, and also in the newspaper occasionally. Look at a news report and specifically the business section. Heck, look at page one. There you will see that Company X has just announced a layoff of 20 percent of its work force! Company Y has announced a RIF (reduction is force—another one in two years, mind you). Company Z had plans to merge with Company A resulting in the omission of overlapping marketing, accounting and research functions. Company B filed for Chapter 11 bankruptcy. Company C announced plans to go-to-market via a distributor sales force and cut 54 percent of its sales organization. It goes on and on and on.

And, now turn to the stock page of the paper and notice that all of these companies are seeing gains in their stock prices! This activity reinforces that the CEO gets paid to please the stockholders before stakeholders and certainly before employees. So, who is left when these things occur? It is the ones offering the most successful qualities—the ones who can bring everlasting value. In short, it is the successful ones.

But not always. It is never that cut and dry. Read some annual stock reports or 10K reports, and you will see much more than just performance results. There is a lot of forward guidance in those narratives. Things like this are public knowledge (at least in business circles): a major international pharma company instituted a multi-year rolling layoff program aimed at reducing its personnel and therefore costs. This, in large part was due to its burgeoning work force via acquisitions. This RIF consisted of one criteria; reduce redundancy. Consequently, a list of names was circulated every other Friday, and if your name appeared on it, you were terminated on the spot. My middle son, Tony hit the list after seven years of dutiful and progressively more challenging work, the highest possible ratings, and the attainment of a full-blown company paid for Master's degree in finance. Thank you and bye-bye.

Quickly he enacted a game plan for the future and it went something like this (Speaking businessorally): Tony knew via his personal SWOT that his core competency revolved around financial policies and regulations (strength). He kept his skills sharp and up to date via the recently acquired MBA in finance (strength). Remaining dogged and persistent (aggressive) he planned for a successful job campaign (threat). Tony remained proactive and positive in discerning openings and enlisted the support of trusted business associates while building a personal network (weakness). The top priority via his team input was to connect the dots and focus on the position—be it permanent or temporary—and to forgo salary as the driving factor (opportunity). Another tactic was keeping everyone in the loop, including recruiters, personal team, past co-workers, and family. He was vigilant to send status updates and notes of thanks to all involved, and tirelessly thought through all scenarios. After two consulting assignments where he applied his skills and learned an innovative program, he parlayed his up-to-date experience and accepted a permanent position with higher pay and stature than the previous employer offered.

Thankfully, this enterprising young professional persevered because he had thought about his future and practiced continuous improvement principles. He hatched and enacted a plan that resulted in an even better position. Knowing full well that the days of thirty years and the gold watch are probably a thing of the past, he entered into this new phase of his life with a positive outlook and guiding principles.

Success came as a result of good planning, established core competencies, and ardent focusing on the conquest that a new venture would bring. He made success an urgent matter! Tony's foundation is solid, and so is he.

This real-life scenario really speaks to the notion that it is not enough to be successful, as success is indeed fleeting. It cries out to the necessity of having lasting and perpetual success to compete in the twenty-first century business world. Try taking these twelve traits and adding "-ing" to the critical behavior in each to make them actionable. That's exactly what my son did. Give it a test run yourself; remember, your elevator ride is just around the corner.

There is of course, an alternative, though it's not very pleasant. It involves being a passive spectator in life rather than an active participant. The path of least resistance is to just let things happen to you, and react to the circumstances of life instead of purposely going after what you want, and having a well thought out plan to get there. It leads to failure and a lot of frustration, but it's always an option (an awful one!) for those who don't want to give it their all to make it in the world of business, and be a winner in the game of life. As one of America's foremost business philosophers, Jim Rohn aptly professed, "One must connive their own life plan lest you be a small part of someone else's plan."

. . .

To my father, Pop, the top three things that made him successful were his ability to be an early adapter of the newest trends, his forward leaning posture and his unique ability to learn from others while teaching himself.

So, my fatherly advice:

- Accelerate the development of your secondary and tertiary core competencies.

- Develop your personal success quotation. Begin living it.

- Become your own visionary of success. Map it out; see it; feel it.

- Conduct a character check on yourself. How you doing?

- Is your posture such that every business encounter is positive?

Let's converse about being competent and understanding the concept of trial and triumph while using the art of conversation to attain lofty goals in your business life.

7

It's All About
Being Competent

"In the end, all business operations can be reduced to three words: people, product and profits.
Unless you've got a good team,
you can't do much with the other two."

Lee Iacocca

Pop's impressive business acumen was mostly predicated on his innate ability to plan, communicate, and lead by example. Everything else he needed to be successful he had to teach himself. Calling him competent would be an understatement. What would your peers and/or subordinates say about you? Let's talk about how competent you are.

COMPETENT. Capable, able, experienced, talented—call it what you will, but employers really want to answer only one central question: how competent is this individual? Each time you are reviewed, the critical question remains: how competent is this individual? Being considered for a promotion: how competent is this individual? A special assignment opportunity comes up, a task force is born, interdepartmental demands require outside thinking, a crisis suddenly appears and myriad other initiatives, problems, and opportunities arise in companies all the time. That same key question is always right there at the heart of the matter.

If you're not being asked to participate in new challenges, you'd better begin looking for another job! The reason is that you lack the competencies to take the reins of any of these initiatives. Oh, you may have some value, but I would venture to say that it is dwindling all the time as companies continually pare their balance sheets and are asking (i.e., demanding) more of their employees than ever before.

Streamlining, flattening, or decentralizing are standard operating procedure in today's business world, so realize that your days are numbered unless you can demonstrate multiple competencies. There quite literally is no other way if you ever hope to move up, run a division, or assist the leaders in taking the company to another level. Remember, you need to be rehired time and time again in your company and most likely the next company and the one after that. Are you up for the challenge?

Let's start at the beginning. To be successful adopt the principle of carefully selecting the individuals with whom you work, and surround yourself with good people. Hiring managers strive to do just that. They must answer "yes" to key hiring questions just as if they owned the company. In essence, hiring managers spend their recruitment funds wisely to bring in talent that will eventually make the company more money. It's called Return on Investment (ROI). Hiring the right work force is one of the biggest and most important investments a company can make. It doesn't get any simpler than that.

To be honest, you passed that test the day you were offered and accepted your current position. Of course, the tests are constant and more challenging the higher you ride the corporate elevator.

Furthermore, be mindful that you also have superiors, and you are surrounded by swarms of co-workers from managers to peers and possibly subordinates. You may be part of a cross-matrixed working relationship where you will input into another person's performance evaluation but have no direct control over them. On the other hand, you may be the recipient of such supervision. And let us not forget about HR, legal, sales, manufacturing, IT, finance, and other allied departments you come in contact with as some people are above and some are below you in the company's hierarchy. There is also the company administrative staff, the custodians as well as the security detail and the landscape crew and so on. From outside the company you may deal with consultants and vendors. One day you may be in charge of some of those teams and your management styles will surely be tested so don't forget for a minute that everyone you come in contact with is sizing you up asking the same questions you are of them. For certain, no one ever knows where or when the merry-go-round stops and just exactly where you will be in the jungle of corporate life.

Here are the key hiring questions that should be applied to any and all hiring scenarios:

- Would you spend your personal money to hire this person?

- On make-or-break projects would you work with this person?

- Someday would you work for this person?

If the answers to these questions are negative, then another candidate should be considered for the position. Moreover, consider this: what are the candidates being measured against if nothing more than against each other? I hope to goodness it is against accumulated competencies needed to do the job and do it well at a minimum. After all, do you want to be surrounded by people who are just nominally better than the rejected candidates, that is, the best of the rest, or do you want to be surrounded by the best money can buy?

Subconsciously, you make these judgments all the time, especially when examining those above you in the pecking order. You do this to gauge your worth to the company, and this barometer serves as your measuring stick against your perceived competitors for the next assignment. Graded too softly and complacency can set in; too harshly and the result can be paralysis. In any event, this measure grates on you daily as it becomes the measure above all measures as you seek to know what people really think of you. In an odd sort of way, this should be mildly motivating. It really is a jungle out there, so if you don't want to get eaten alive, stay hungry.

• • •

So how does all this matter in the larger scope of the business world? How (and how much!) do you really matter to the team, the work community, and the entire organization? How do others measure up to you and your standards and principles? How do you really know you are surrounding yourself with good people?

The answer—no big surprise here if you've been paying attention—is an individual's competence. Yes, acquired competencies against an array of defined associated skills set you apart from the crowd. It is against these competencies (below) that hiring decisions are made, and they should be the measures against which you select the people with whom you surround yourself.

Here is a basic competency model developed by observing and working with and for highly successful people. The ten most compulsory competencies are the following:

1. INITIATIVE

2. RESOURCEFULNESS

3. PLANNING

4. COMMUNICATION

5. LEADERSHIP

6. MANAGEMENT ACCOUNTABILITY

7. NEGOTIATION

8. CONTINUOUS IMPROVEMENT

9. INTERPERSONAL ABILITY

10. COMMUNAL AWARENESS

Individual competencies are presented with crucial queries against essential and demonstrated behaviors. It would not be surprising that you are currently being measured against some of these competencies. At least I hope so, for in a unique way having high standards is one factor with which to evaluate the strength of a company. Think about it: would you rather work for a firm that accepts mediocre performance or one that stretches their people to attain loftier goals? Grade yourself and see just how competent you are. Then picture a teammate or boss and grade them. Where do you stand on the bar chart relative to your peers and your superiors? How competent are you? Thank goodness the process is iterative. Check back over a period of time to ensure personal progress.

Competencies

INITIATIVE
Proactively Works to Improve Oneself
and the Organization

Those with initiative can spark a thought and carry the load when left unsupervised. These are the self-starters in new as well as familiar tasks. They are counted on "to be there" always! They demonstrate a proactive as opposed to a reactive posture. These are the challenge seekers. Any organization would quickly stagnate without them. It all starts here.

Crucial Queries:

- To what degree does this person need to be told what to do?
- Absent management, can you rely on this person to guide himself?
- To what extent are desire and passion demonstrated?

Continued ...

INITIATIVE
Proactively Works to Improve Oneself and the Organization

Think about It:

If you won't do it, who will is a good place to start when thinking about initiative. Industrious and hardworking also works. But does active, busy and/or diligent really describe someone who displays initiative? The accent here is on "competencies" and not "energy." Urgency should factor in.

Think, Even When It Hurts:

- Which competencies do you favor in yourself, your co-workers, your superiors, and your hires—industrious vs. busy; hardworking vs. diligent?
- Money, as in an investment, is being spent to bring value to the team—have you demonstrated your value? It takes initiative to do that. Does it feel urgent to you?
- Where do you grade yourself, peers, and superiors with regard to initiative?

RESOURCEFULNESS
Display Ingenuity; Question Incisively

Finding a way to "make things happen" defines this skill. Resourceful people develop networks to enable the team to continually move forward. They are perpetual learners who anticipate pitfalls and negotiate ahead of trouble. They eliminate downtime; they question with an acute purpose. They interminably pursue innovation and are vigorously inquisitive.

Crucial Queries:

- Does this person demonstrate a quick learning curve?
- Do unexpected events stop progress or can this person hit the curve ball?
- Can this person identify the ingredients when there is no recipe?

Continued ...

RESOURCEFULNESS
Display Ingenuity; Question Incisively

Think about It:

To be resourceful is to be mindful of both personal and team goals. One must perceive trends, problems and opportunities from various sources to identify alternative operating strategies. Upon recognizing ineffective practices one routinely offers innovative solutions. A resourceful person questions and enquires for continuous personal and team development.

Think, Even When It Hurts:

- Instead of acting (emphasis on "acting") like a genius try being ingenious. Be humbly resourceful.
- Resourcefulness and purposeful posture are inseparable.
- Where do you grade yourself, peers, and superiors with regard to resourcefulness?

PLANNING
Apply Innovative Approaches
to Business Situations

Planners provide a sense of direction and harmony. They display both a long and short-term vision for successfully completing project plans related to time savings and efficient and effective work. They are able to evaluate problematic situations and resolve them with logic and sound judgment in a collaborative way. Good planners are grounded in continuous improvement principles.

Crucial Queries:

- Are plans documented, discussed, revised, and revisited on a continual basis, that is, does an iterative planning process exist?
- Are plans action oriented with backup ideas and contingencies?
- If derailed, do you have a realistic means of getting back on track?
- Are key milestones identified, and does the plan lead to results? Are goals met?

Continued ...

PLANNING
Apply Innovative Approaches
to Business Situations

Think about It:

Planning is first and foremost directional in nature. Due to its goal setting component, good planning avoids potential career and organizational heartache. Successful plans are "action" oriented and executional. Secondary, tertiary, and contingency plans must exist. Why plan if you don't execute?

Think Even When It Hurts:

- Can you prioritize, and do you have a plan for where you are going?
- Can you translate modern technology into actionable solutions?
- Where do you grade yourself, peers and superiors with regard to planning skills?

COMMUNICATION
All Forms of It
Are Clear, Concise, Persuasive and Impactful

Adept communicators focus on clarity and succinctness to get positive results in internal and external exchanges. They can vary delivery to the situation. They can summarize complex information to elicit meaningful dialog. Brevity is the hallmark of good business communications. The best communicators listen actively and respond convincingly.

Crucial Queries:

- Are communications consistently applied? Are others actively listening? Is there a hint of persuasion in your communications?
- Is all written expression concise, understandable, and grammatically correct? Is oral delivery void of "ha," "umm," "like," and all slang?
- Can you lead or follow complex dialogue?

Continued ...

COMMUNICATION
All Forms of It
Are Clear, Concise, Persuasive and Impactful

Think about It:

Effective presentations are delivered by succinctly getting to the crux of an issue. Understand everyone's "time demands," so make exchanges brief. Active listeners think before speaking. They elicit positive responses. Use a closing "call for action" in communications when necessary.

Think Even When It Hurts:

- Think of communications as your face on a piece of paper. Like it?
- Practice this crucial skill until you are proficient. Think of it as your first and only chance to make a first impression . . . each and every time.
- Where do you grade yourself, peers and superiors with regard to communication skills?

LEADERSHIP
Naturally Has a Following

Leaders can and willingly act with a sense of purpose and ownership. They evoke images of what is possible and doable; they rally people around concepts and ideas. Leaders focus people's minds on what is desirable, possible, and necessary. They get passionate about goal setting. They covet the opportunity to "make a difference." They boldly determine the direction a business takes.

Crucial Queries:

- Who is sought after when at the water cooler? Do people follow one person willingly? When she turns around, is someone following her?
- Does this person command the respect of teammates, superiors, and subordinates as well as clients and vendors?
- Would you choose this person to represent you and/or your team in important client meetings?

Continued ...

LEADERSHIP
Naturally Has a Following

Think about It:

Leadership inevitably requires using power to influence the thoughts and actions of others. Leaders are active, not reactive; they shape ideas instead of responding to them. They adopt a personal attitude toward goals. Leaders retain responsibility after delegating authority.

Think Even When It Hurts:

- Think of leadership in terms of persistence, tough-mindedness, intelligence, analytical ability and most importantly tolerance and good will. How about you; do you have these traits?
- Where do you grade yourself, peers and superiors with regard to leadership skills?

MANAGEMENT ACCOUNTABILITY
Demonstrates Total Ownership

These people accept and "own" management's decisions. They remain team players even when their views are in the minority. They contribute to the larger goal at all times. One who is accountable accepts constructive critiques and demonstrates professionalism when leading or following. This is one of the more critical abilities, as it demonstrates the individual "gets it."

Crucial Queries:

- Are actions really louder than words?
- Is there personal responsibility and accountability for all decisions and business outcomes?
- Does loyalty resonate with the company and not just to an individual?

Continued ...

MANAGEMENT ACCOUNTABILITY
Demonstrates Total Ownership

Think about It:

Management accountability often times equates with personal sacrifice. Do you have to be led all the time? Is doing the right thing the same as doing your thing? Do you know the difference between leading, following, and getting out of the way and when to adopt each one? Are you concerned with popularity; are you open to constructive feedback?

Think Even When It Hurts:

- Do you conduct self-critiques? The resulting perspective provides redemption.
- What is more important, your goals or the company goals?
- Where do you grade yourself, peers and superiors with regard to management accountability skills?

NEGOTIATION
Conducts Appropriate and Professional Relations with Empathy

Negotiation requires one to possess the ability to find the middle ground because it is the right place to be. Negotiators clearly perform in the mode of "if I do this for you, will you do this for me?" This requires alignment with the "win-win" philosophy, avoiding "lose-lose" situations and knowing when to win-lose/lose-win to keep relationships moving forward.

Crucial Queries:

- Are good working relationships maintained with team members, superiors and clients at all times, in all settings, and in a professional manner?
- Are individual and company reputation enhanced and not tarnished for having participated in the encounter?
- Is it wise to give an inch to gain a yard?

Continued ...

NEGOTIATION
Conducts Appropriate and Professional Relations with Empathy

Think about It:

Negotiations are meant as a give and take as both sides realize change is happening. Relationships must be left intact if both want to move the process forward now and into the future. Long-term implications are top of mind with resulting agreements. Planning skills enhance negotiation skills.

Think Even When It Hurts:

- Are you engaged or engaging? Can you anticipate another's needs?
- Are you always invited back for conversation and possible contribution?
- Where do you grade yourself, peers and superiors with regard to negotiation skills?

CONTINUOUS IMPROVEMENT
Living in the Inquiry Mode

All those seeking to make things better, more efficient, and more effective live in this mode. Subscribers develop an inquisitive mindset and never lose their constant gaze of inquiry. They demonstrate a three-dimensional view of all situations, opportunities, and problems. They advocate for questions to answers seeking a mandate for continual positive transformation. Continuous improvement is the impetus for organic growth.

Crucial Queries:

- To what extent are you and your team inquisitive? Is self-improvement a routine way of doing business?
- Do you contribute in areas not of your specialty? Do team members venture out of comfort zones to find new ways of operating?
- Be affected by change or be the face of change, but things will change. Answer how did it happen or question it until it becomes praiseworthy.

Continued ...

CONTINUOUS IMPROVEMENT
Living in the Inquiry Mode

Think about It:

Philosophies will change; adopt them. Better yet, lead them. Improve constantly and forever via education, reflection, perspective, and redemption. Rarely is organic growth at the ready, but in continuous improvement it's free yet valuable. Transformation equals revitalization.

Think Even When It Hurts:

- Instead of trying to have all the answers, try having pertinent questions.
- Where do you grade yourself, peers and superiors with regard to continuous improvement?

INTERPERSONAL ABILITY
Fostering and Maintaining Positive Relationships

To be proficient in this competency is to act with humility and dignity while being sensitive, tactful, and considerate. Commanding genuine respect to cultivate constructive partnerships is its goal. Being mindful of the "turning point" aspect of every encounter, this person accents the positive outcomes of all encounters. Tact, diplomacy, and objectivity are evident.

Crucial Queries

- Do you act in a nonthreatening manner? Are you respected, not feared, welcomed, and wanted?
- Do you remain perceptive while being persistent and persevering?
- Do you accept yes with gratitude and respect? Do you act with compassion and sensitivity, knowing when to say no?

Continued ...

INTERPERSONAL ABILITY
Fostering and Maintaining Positive Relationships

Think about It:

You only get one chance to make a first impression; in business you will be measured on all subsequent chances too. The hole that is dug from a miss on the first one is deep in business, almost fatal. Be ready via ardent preparation. Stick with facts; interact in an open and modest manner.

Think Even When It Hurts:

- Interpersonal ability aligns with communications. Mastering one is like a two for one sale.
- Where do you grade yourself, peers and superiors with regard to interpersonal ability?

COMMUNAL AWARENESS
Knowledgeable of the Larger Goals

This competency is demonstrated via an awareness of the company's total business. Proficiency equates to understanding company objectives by aligning plans with them. Recognizing the financial impact of decisions is a key measure. One must be current with external forces affecting the business, that is, competition, customers, vendors, regulatory agencies, and community.

Crucial Queries

- Are strategic endeavors aligned to corporate financial goals?
- Is Return on Investment a part of the strategy?
- Can you name the top threat to success at all times? Are there contingency plans for all actions?

Continued ...

COMMUNAL AWARENESS
Knowledgeable of the Larger Goals

Think about It:

Do you have an established network of positive working relationships? Can you assimilate other's perspectives and ideas to achieve objectives? Is your knowledge of interrelated departments sufficient to affect business outcomes? Are your plans aligned to larger goals?

Think Even When It Hurts:

- Are you organizationally astute? Consider it a long term objective.
- Do you consider the long-term implications of all business decisions?
- Where do you grade yourself, peers and superiors with regard to Communal Awareness?

• • •

Yes, being competent is the true measure of any professional. Gauging competencies requires careful observation as well as tangible demonstration of such competency. They should be applied consistently and be obvious to everyone. Highly developed competencies are to be emulated, and as with leadership, when applied routinely, everyone will follow this person. At a minimum, highly competent individuals will raise the bar for others, thereby making the team a better organization. A good mentor teaches against advanced competencies all the while imitating them to demonstrate their principles. Keep asking yourself, how many people are following you and picking up on your lead?

The better organizations are filled with competent people across the board. Recruiters recruit exclusively from them. Top-tier schools have candidates laser focused on them from day one. Corporate leaders emerge from the competitive landscape that they create. In short, working in an environment of competent people is the essence of continuous improvement and proves its very essence.

In growing, leading-edge companies you must add advancement potential, and in even more complex and emerging market situations, nothing but highly competent and competitive people will do. Acquiring higher level competencies such as business integration, management direction, and versatility is mandatory if you are to reach the apex of a challenging career.

The bottom line is what you are measured on and what you should measure others on rests in this simple and prevailing question: just how competent are you?

Famous business leader, Automotive Hall of Famer and the father of the Ford Mustang, Lee Iacocca mused that a good team of people outranks products and profits every time. To emphasize this, I like to ask, just as he did, "How competent are you?" How competent is your team?"

Do you think that the effort to become more competent is a worthy exercise? Are you challenged to change or improve your station in life? Perhaps a little motivation from Saint Francis would help you jump start an internal discussion: "*Do what you have always done; get what you have always gotten.*" Think about it! And, if you conclude that you are happy, ask yourself this: are you really just complacent?

• • •

To my father, Pop, the top three competencies he exhibited were planning, communicating, and leading by example. He made himself better through introspection. He benchmarked against what he thought were better business people than himself. We talked about this a great deal. I believe by talking out loud he learned a lot. He was a master at practicing what he preached. He was far more competent than he knew.

So, my fatherly advice:

• What are your top three personal competencies? Summon some internal perspective and begin redemption toward two competencies that need addressing. Is this aspect of your development in your personal game plan?

- Revisit your personal SWOT. See any weaknesses that you may have missed. Any strengths to play off? Sketch out a future SWOT, say one year from now and get working on it. This is painless for continuous improvement subscribers.

- How do these competencies stack up against what you are measured on currently? Should you address all of them? Can you add to them?

- Realizing you must have at least one sustainable indispensable competency, develop a secondary one by combining strengths and opportunities from your competency SWOT.

- If you owned a business, would you hire you?

Let's converse about the concept of trial and triumph while using the art of conversation to attain lofty goals in your business life.

8

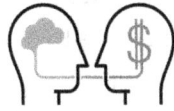

Goals
Expectations

*"Your focus needs to be on your goals and desires,
rather than your fears and worries."*

Nishchal Ningleku

Pop adroitly focused on his goals, determined to manage a successful business. He had no fear of failure; he worried only about the things he could control. Unemployment had reached 25 percent in his era, but somehow confidence and optimism were infused family traits. Perseverance and sacrifice were adopted attitudes, not slogans. He expected nothing but planned for everything. He saw what the bottom looked like; he dreamt of just the opposite. He made it a goal to be successful. Let's talk about the difference between goals and expectations.

GOALS. Goals are palpable and concrete desires that can be measured and benchmarked. Goals are inherently *"set"* to make things better. They are original by nature. They provide the altimeter to measure travel to new heights. Goals can be finite measures, incremental plans, and even stepping stones. They are almost elusive if they are to be valued. Easy and effortless are anathema when it comes to goal setting. Challenge and determination define their very existence. Think of the football sailing through the *goal* posts; the soccer ball crossing the *goal* line, or the hockey puck going into the netted *goal*. Goals, when achieved, are what the checkered flag is to the finish line—victory over apathy, action over inaction, and triumph over tribulation. Make it a goal to set goals.

Don't misinterpret goals for dreams. Dreams are largely uncontrollable events as they occur usually during sleep. Goals have targeted consequences. You don't have to sit around and hope for them to happen—you can actually *make* them a reality. Dreamers are the people we often sneer at, while goal driven people are admired and emulated. Dare not to dream; dream to dare yourself to reach new heights. Accept the challenge! Dreaming, for the most part, is backward-looking; goal setting is always about the future. Think about how you will spend your goal-driven rewards, then continually set new goals by raising the bar.

EXPECTATIONS. Anticipation, probability, or even luck could define this conscious sentiment. Sadly, and in most nonbusiness activities, establishing expectations is often little more than indulging in wistful imaginary musings. Chance, more than anything, defines the word. In business, however, the word *expectations* could and does have a different perspective as you will see.

Personal expectations differ from goals in that they are intangible, dreamlike cravings by their very nature. They are seldom if ever measured. There is no way to benchmark against progress for there is no established path to work against. You really can't achieve an expectation. Little if any energy is spent on developing personal expectations. Hope rules this phenomenon. Fantasy drives its existence. Capricious musings provide unrealistic images of joyful accomplishments, celebratory achievements, and even ultimate success. They flat out do not exist and are, in fact, just delusional daydreams.

In business, just as complacency is tantamount to corporate death, "expecting" a promotion or a raise is synonymous with acerbic disappointment. Save the dreaming for when you are asleep. Replace it with goal setting in all business endeavors.

Make the crucial distinction between setting a goal and having an expectation. When Apple began marketing the Apple Watch, consumers may have expected large lines in front of Apple stores typical of an iPhone release. In reality Apple scrapped that idea in order to achieve its goals. The tech giant also scaled down the launch to just one-third of the countries for the iPhones launch, and they also eschewed most other retail outlets opting for more control via Apple retail outlets almost exclusively. For the first time they began to tailor their approach by inviting potential customers to try the watch to generate interest. The change in tactics supports the overall strategy to lay the groundwork for a successful introduction of the watch. Apple didn't expect the watch to rival sales of the iPhone, the objective being a new entry into the luxury watch market. The goal remains for the watch to be a profitable new item in the Apple arsenal. As sales reports began to flow in, profit expectations as well as marketing, inventory, and distribution systems were adjusted to ensure the goal of introducing a profitable new luxury item was accomplished.

Here in one example, Apple demonstrates its solid understanding of goals and expectations. More importantly, they understand their customers' expectation level and incorporate it into the goal-setting process. Perfect.

• • •

The most blatant difference between striving for a goal and expecting something is in the eventual outcome. One result could be extreme euphoria while the other is nearly always extreme disappointment. Guess which one is a goal and which one is an expectation? Apple knows!

Back to the football kicker—did the football kicker expect to make the field goal or did he set intermediate goals for himself leading up to being confident enough to expect making that kick? He had to master a repeatable technique, increase his power, and perfect his form all in an effort to make a twenty-five-yard field goal; then the forty yarder became the aim, up and until splitting the uprights with the winning, record-setting seventy-two-yard Super Bowl kick became the goal! Yes, it may have begun as a dream, but only after all the practice and attainment of many intermediary goals, does the kicker expect to make the kick? Indeed, at some point goals and expectations do serve one another well. Understanding which is which is the trick.

Think about some of the many concepts you've learned so far. Can you see that knowing what matters is really important? Can you see now how a positive posture relates to goal setting?

Goals

Goal setting really is a subset of continuous improvement. And, how about work, defined as energy focused on a task? Can you see that it will take work to formulate goals? How about competencies relative to perpetual success? Do you think successful people are goal setters? Perhaps goal setting should be included among the traits adopted by competent and successful people. I believe it is an inherently accepted trait of perpetually successful people. It's worth repeating: make it a goal to set goals.

Yes, without goals one could wander aimlessly through life with little hope for personal satisfaction. Pick one of the following happenings: Imagine expecting to win a Super Bowl. Imagine expecting to receive your company's best performer award. Imagine expecting to be president of the company you work for. Imagine expecting nothing.

Did you catch that last one? It is the only possible real outcome of any expectation. Expect nothing. Plan for anything; work for everything—even an outstanding career. Why not?

So, what's the lesson you ask? It's really important to take a good hearty look at the things you desire in life and in business and clearly categorize them as either goals or expectations. The distinctively emotional nature of expectations makes them convenient gauges, but goals ensure you are working on getting there. Try keeping your goals foremost in your mind and your expectations for your next birthday present—your aspirations will thank you more than you can believe.

• • •

How does all this matter in the larger scope of the business world?

The business landscape is full of examples of how goal setting was the key factor in attaining new heights. Realizing a dominant market share is a goal worthy of achieving. Lowering costs, extending brand lines, raising the collective intelligence of the workforce, acquiring and divesting, and entering new markets are other business goals. The list goes on and on. Making the quarterly earnings per share (EPS) number is a major goal shared by many stock exchange listed companies (EPS = net income / average outstanding common shares). It is a precisely examined metric that is often used as a barometer to gauge a company's profitability per unit of shareholder ownership. Earnings per share is a key driver of share price yet it is one of many measures for the investing community to evaluate. IBM, for example, has set a goal for future EPS for quite some time. In effect, it is a well-regarded corporate target. Without targets, a company cannot grow. And growing the company relates directly to companies striving to attain or maintain a sustainable competitive advantage.

Sometimes expectations are established by outside influences. The best example is how Wall Street analysts sets the future earnings estimate for companies to reach. Many factors contribute to the forecasting model, but alas, an expected number to reach is out there quarter after quarter.

At first, measures such as EPS and earnings estimates raise expectations. Just by stating them, they become targets—goals if you will. It comes with the territory. In essence, these numbers are sometimes a goal and sometimes an expectation.

Goals

If either the goals or the expectations are not achieved, there will be consequences. The price for failing to realize either number is often times paid in the company's stock price where inevitably it retreats regardless of whether all other leading indicators are positive. Meeting benchmarks has become the measuring stick for CEOs of all companies. The adopted tactic for the CEO is to set goals toward making the number. The iterative business plan is tweaked and tweaked once again, reset and reset, and fine-tuned constantly. Milestones are benchmarked, adjustments are made, and action and resultant reaction tumble daily on the competitive battlefield. The stakes are high—both personally and corporately. Stakeholders and shareholders anxiously anticipate the *number*. The cycle goes on and on and on, and it never stops. The learning here is that the CEO sets goals as the benchmarks that are, in some cases, already set for her. She may have had no input into the number; she just has to achieve it. Providing goals for the company's workforce is largely the job of the CEO, and it is the driving force behind all major decisions. Understanding the ultimate company goal allows all employees to garner much needed perspective. Divisional, regional, unit, and personal goals all in some way shape, form, or tie into the larger company goal, and while they may not be shared directly, everything hinges on making the number—quarter after quarter.

Yes, it is all about competition, and thank goodness you have some. It is the competitive nature of business that makes us grow. If you thought fear was a motivator, well, how about missing the number! Make no mistake; we all have numbers to hit. Constantly.

On the personnel side of the business, employees must continually strive to better themselves if we are to compete in the business world. Here the word "expectations" has meaning—true meaning for in many companies expectations are predetermined as in minimal, base-line measurements one must achieve to either stay in the fold or progress up the ranks. Meeting expectations may get you to another pay period (all other things being equal) but why on earth would you want to settle for that? Exceeding expectations begins to set you apart. Let's not even talk about performances that are below expectations. Here, as was with the CEO, expectations are largely established for you—no need to fret about them. Your job, just as it is the collective company's job, is to set goals so as to achieve them and, even more critically, to exceed every expectation.

• • •

The question now becomes, "How do I do that—exceed expectations?" As you can imagine, the answer lies in setting goals to ensure you are working toward exceeding expectations. Oh, as if it was just that easy! But perhaps it is easier than you might expect. Just revisit previous chapters for insight. Understanding the principles of knowing what matters and continuous improvement is a good place to start. Layer in some good old-fashioned focus with a positive posture, some initiative, ardent planning, and personal accountability, and the rest will come naturally and easily. All that's left is a system to help ensure you are on your way.

Here's a process that while it oftentimes confounds it is really straightforward and employed time and time again in the business world. There is no real name for it, and while posed as a process, it really is a system, and here's something that probably won't surprise you: it is all about the system! None other than the guru of continuous improvement principles, the renowned Dr. W. Edwards Deming himself proclaims, "A bad system will beat a good person every time." His message to us is to be clear on your approach to problem solving, inventions, and initiatives by focusing on a positive outcome. Here are four tenets making up a formula to execute a successful mission. It is often referred to as GOST:

GOALS

OBJECTIVES

STRATEGIES

TACTICS

Let's break this formula down. While it is not necessarily universally applied in all business circles, some elements reside in every plan from exhaustive multi-year, multi-faceted business plans to your personal growth and development plan. Yet, the words—and more importantly, the concepts—behind those words provide real meaning and act as a foundational approach to problem solving. Understanding them and their importance in the formula is critical if you are to merge actions with plans thus ensuring their warranted execution. Let's define each step for understanding:

GOALS: A declarative and usually broad statement that has a primary outcome. Goals serve to drive strategic planning. The goal provides general direction but is rarely accompanied by a defining metric. It simply answers *what* is to be accomplished as opposed to how you will accomplish it. Simply put, *it's the big idea*. If there is a bigger idea you can usually find it in the company's mission statement. It is the ultimate accomplishment. Goals are supported by measurable objectives.

OBJECTIVES: Objectives and goals are closely aligned and practically interchangeable. Think of objectives as sub-goals as there can be many of them but usually only one main goal. An objective is specific and measureable while stated to achieve the goal. Objectives usually begin with an action word or verb and often contain numbers. They render goals self-fulfilling as they answer "*what and when.*" Principally quantitative, objectives are the most impactful of the elements in the system. They address how much will be accomplished.

STRATEGIES: The *plan* for all practical purposes, strategies are "*how*" you are going to execute against the objectives. Strategies are schematically focused, distinct, and somewhat conceptual action plans. They address the methods, set the expectations, and provide the compass by which the objective is achieved. Strategies are general as opposed to tactical in scope. Tactics are needed to actualize the objectives.

TACTICS: Tactics define the strategies. They are specific actions to implement the strategies thus achieving the objectives. There are usually many tactics addressing all the sub-goals, objectives, and strategies. "By when" often accompanies every tactic. Closure is near by their very nature, although the element of time needs to be expressed for the tactics to be coordinated effectively. If the "devil is in the details," *tactic* is Satan.

How about a picture to sum it up? The goal is to create a modern train system, the objective of which is to be the fastest by 20 percent. The strategy is the scientifically controlled self-driving engine that propels it, while the detailed tactics are compartmentalized in the caboose.

The GOST formula is really an inverted pyramid of sorts. It is very broad at the top (as in a far-reaching statement) and very narrow at the bottom (streamlined actions). It is intentionally built that way as it is the drill-down effect that drives toward an eventual positive outcome. However, in its executional phase it resembles the historic depiction of the pyramid in that the base or tactical plank acts as a wide foundation to which layered above are the strategies that hold up objectives in an attempt to achieve the singular goal. It goes both ways, just as goals and expectations do. Knowing the difference and outcomes of each is the trick. It's all about the system!

Of course, all of this has little meaning without execution. Execution is critical to the success of any endeavor. Execution is the key to being competitive.

Understanding the process of executing plans rounds out the system of planning for successful missions. Execution requires disciplined adherence to a process of associated activities to enable a strategy to work. As I mentioned before, planning without execution is merely an exercise in futility. And, just because an execution process is formulated, success is not guaranteed. As the widely acclaimed, father of business management, Peter Drucker states, *"Plans are only good intentions unless they immediately degenerate into hard work."* And, as you know, work is energy focused on a task.

Yes, this step is vitally important in your quest to attain your goals. Bear in mind, of course, most of us are trained to plan;

not execute. As the tag line of this very book claims, you don't necessarily learn everything in college. How could you? Perspective is sorely lacking at that juncture in your business life. Learning to plan is a step up and a real value to younger business folks, so we learn, among other things, the core elements of marketing research to gain insight and understanding. We apply that to market a make-believe product. We take our *As* and *Bs*, pat ourselves on the back, and move on toward graduation. However, you never get the chance to enact those ideas, never see them to fruition. You are graded on planning; not executing. And, that's OK until you finally get the opportunity do it for real.

Key elements in the execution phase contain some basic ingredients. Paramount among them is the understanding that planning and execution are not incongruent activities. To enhance the success quotient, these two undertakings should be done simultaneously. The execution phase will require more time than the planning phase. Time will also change depending on market developments, competitive reactions, government compulsions, and mandated corporate initiatives. *There is never enough time* and *now is not the right time* are two time constraints one must fight through to successfully execute any plan.

Execution, while purposely aligned with planning, is its own process and not just another step in another process. It augments the planning process. Take it from Mike Roach, CEO of CGI, a 31, 000 person IT firm as he states, "Strategy without execution is hallucination!"

The only word containing the letter *u* as in *you* is in the final stage: exec*u*tion. Finish it off; own the total system. It will make you a better business planner, a better business communicator, and a better business person—period.

Reformulated, the "GOSTE" system now looks like this:

GOALS

OBJECTIVES

STRATEGIES

TACTICS

EXECUTION

As Pop used to do with me, let's step away from business to see just what the goal setting process is all about. His army duty being that of a communications intelligence specialist, he often used the war theme to get his message across. And since the business landscape is likened to war in many aspects let's use the war metaphor as a way to illustrate its understanding:

Goal: *Win the war.*

In and of itself, it's a pretty simple idea. In fact, it's a very broad statement. It seems pretty straightforward. It's declarative and defines an outcome. It's a big idea.

Objective: *Knock out the airfields; command the seas, shutter communications, capture the generals and establish a new government before the up-coming elections.*

The objective directly connects to the goal and is, in fact, of the same vernacular. Many action words are listed within the objective statement, and while no date is firmly set, there is a loose alignment with election season thus a time reference is established and therefore measurable. The objective answers

"what and when" and in so doing it does address how much
will be accomplished.

*Strategy: Begin the Air Force bombing campaigns, position the
Navy battleships and aircraft carriers, and deploy the Army
Rangers, and Marine brigades targeted at major communication
towers along the coastlines.*

The "how" is now established; the scheme is announced and
ready for the next line of management to provide details (tactics). Expectations are set, marching orders (in this case literally) are understood. It is time to get down to brass tacks.

Tactics:

Timing	AIR	SEA	LAND
Phase 1	Deploy Missiles at munitions depots	Warships from the 4th fleet deployed	Deploy trained airborne, anti-aircraft, army and artillery forces
Phase 2	Conduct HQ bombing raids	Aircraft carriers aimed at strategic targets	Attack perimeters, target capital cities
Phase 3	Provide ground cover as needed	Deploy ground troops from landing crafts	Converge at HQ to capture Generals

These tactics directly relate to the strategies. They are unified
against the central goal and specific to the objective. The added
element of "when" is established. The tactics support the entire
operation and speak directly to the execution of the plan.

Execution: *Three central requirements include monitoring of operations, status reports, and enemy response. A communications post needs to be established to ensure command operations function smoothly and all service branches are in cohesive assault mode at all times. Manpower and equipment condition reports are up to-date, replacements readied as are munitions, rations, and support stations.*

As you can see, execution involves more than just "doing it." Execution speaks to not only carrying out the mission but must be all encompassing for everything to work. Execution must be rigid enough to stay the course but swift enough to adapt to conditions on the fly. It is the proverbial fork in the road and sometimes you have to take both roads. Be prepared for the unexpected and be prudent in planning the execution phase.

Now, let's bring it closer to home—or should I say, business. Here's an example from the business world:

GOAL: Make XYZ company the largest seller of retirement planning products.

OBJECTIVES: Educate clients on retirement planning by increasing client participation at IRA lunch and learn sessions.

STRATEGY: Inform clients about all the different retirement vehicles via periodic email blasts.

TACTICS: Email blasts to highlight on a rotational basis IRA, Roth IRA, Traditional IRA and Social Security benefits, rules, cut off dates and taxation issues. Acquire email lists of clients nearing retirement age and no less than 55 years of age. Inform and recruit IRA and securities licensed agents. Contract with luncheon venues. Prepare presentation materials.

EXECUTION: Set up a project template (GANT Chart) to list all duties and events. Track participation vs. invitation. Apply analytics, post results and make adjustments going forward.

I urge you to capture a picture in your mind using GOSTE. This handy reference will act as a guidepost for when the inevitable project is thrown at you with the seemingly perpetual proclamation . . . I need this by COB (close of business) Friday!

. . . and it is Friday, so how about from back in Chapter Two you pick one of your personal items that really matter and get started on making it a reality . . .

GOAL:

_____

_____

_____

_____

OBJECTIVE(s):

_____

_____

_____

_____

STRATEGY(s):

_____

_____

_____

_____

_____

TACTIC(s):

_____

_____

_____

_____

_____

_____

_____

_____

EXECUTION:

_____

_____

_____

_____

_____

_____

_____

From both the business and personal side of the ledger, the lesson to learn is that the process of thinking in a "GOSTEly" way is in fact adroit and geared for results. Understanding and enacting this way of doing business eliminates some of the fear in your mind and rids yourself of needless worries. It addresses the question of "How will I exceed expectations?" Applying the GOSTE mentality to personal goals allows for fervent planning to ensure you are deserving and not just desiring good things to happen. Think about the critical difference between those two! It will assist you in getting on the other side of the equation because you will be constantly working on improving yourself through the attainment of your goals.

As presented in Chapter 5, Working: *Thankfully,* the idea is to be principled and focused while you master a few competencies. Mastering your career goals is the continual challenge. Take heart in the encouraging and inspiring words from poet and management consultant Nishchal Ningleku as he implores you to focus on your goals, not fears; focus on desires, not worries. And, just as in the case with the TPS process, expect to work on concurrent goal setting items. Thank goodness you have become a devotee of continuous improvement!

• • •

To my father, Pop, the top three business goals he worked toward were growing his top line, lowering his expense line, and thereby improving his bottom line, which he referred to as the "living the dream" line.

So, my fatherly advice:

- Study your company's annual report or 10K report and understand the preeminent goal. Ensure you are aligned with its direction.

- Since objectives often times begin with the words "increase" or "improve," try improving your personal output by 10 percent. You can increase it as you go along.

Goals

- Strategies address the "how" part of the equation; how are you living your dream?

- Tactically speaking—sketch out todays goal achieving activities. What others can you add to them?

- Execute everything you plan for, expect nothing, and exceed every expectation.

Finally, let's converse about using the art of conversation to attain lofty goals in your business life. You are about to get into another one of those "elevator" situations. Are you ready to talk about your business?

9

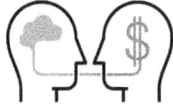

Trial and Triumph
Removal of Pain

"Doing something wrong repeatedly does not make it right."

Tim Fargo

Like any entrepreneur, Pop suffered pain when the business was soft—all kinds of pain: physical, personal, and, of course financial. And, like so many entrepreneurs lacking formal education, mentorships, or any safety net whatsoever, he figured out how to overcome obstacles. His thought was to avoid pain before it reached the acute stage. He could only do it with his will, his stamina, his attitude, and his outlook—that's all he had. And that was good enough. He was all about removing pain by avoiding errors. He knew that errors cost money and without money you cannot eat and if you don't eat you will die. He understood that—fully. To him, it was about being triumphant. That's what he set out to do because to him, since starving is not a very appealing alternative, failure was not an option. Do you have options? Do you think you have options? Let's talk about it.

TRIUMPHANT. In effect, all employees are walking around their virtual world with some degree of self-doubt. Am I doing enough? Am I good enough? Where will I land after the next cut? These questions, while uber-fashionable in the twenty-first century business world, are probably enduring as well. These are the questions that lead to incessant pain. Questions of this nature are synonymous with heartache. If left unchecked they can derail even the most promising of careers. What could be worse than having a twenty-year career when forty years was the goal? What can you do?

So, workers begin trying things to avoid the potentially dire results of a poorly managed career. They enroll in classes to master new subjects. They volunteer for committees to gain insight into new work avenues. They begin networking. They read business articles and books even! They switch careers. They do this and that and more, all in an effort to remain employed so as to eat in order to live. It's called (until now) trial and error. You know, that thing that makes you feel less bad! And, you know what? It's OK. All learning is good learning. But beyond that, being OK is no longer acceptable. It is no longer tolerable. Being OK is yesterday's entitlement mode of operation. Being OK is an error!

The answer to the question "What can you do?" is not to have a parachute, as even golden parachutes are passé. No, the answer is to address the pain prior to its reaching its apex. Proactive thinking or "thinking even when it hurts" is the starting point if you are to avoid the pain associated with (just) being OK.

Having a good understanding of the core concepts you've been introduced to in this book goes a long way in removing pain before it begins. To reiterate, you must know what matters, continuously improve, think critically, work thankfully, and plan on being perpetually successful while being competent at what you do. Etch these concepts into your consciousness, and you will be halfway toward removing potential pain that is inevitably felt by those who are less informed about these concepts. Even better, you will be on your way to full control of your career. These concepts should be central in your business, rather than some of the more commonly held concepts that are seemingly unchallenged because that is simply "the way it is."

• • •

Certain concepts fit nicely into our brains, like supply and demand; time is money; and plan your work, work your plan. These are easily understood and accepted. There is no trial needed and no errors made. You get that "if a certain commodity is in short supply, then the price of that commodity should rise." As an example, take retail gasoline prices. For as long as I can remember prices have always fluctuated based on the supply as the news reporter tells us. Really? Are consumers really that gullible? Where does petroleum come from so that as the supply goes low, prices rise at the pump? He never mentions it; it just happens, and we go and pay at the pump. We get it—it is supply and demand! Using this logic, it is completely possible that the supply could go to zero, and we will never drive gasoline-based cars again. Never! Then one day retail prices go down. We rejoice! What happened to the supply? Isn't this the same resource that was in short supply a little while ago?

It doesn't take a devotee of continuous improvement to ask, "What gives?" This concept illustrates that we almost unconsciously accept the notion that retail gasoline prices will always be whatever they are due to supply and demand. Chalk it up to how smart we are; it's the established concept of supply and demand.

Another easily understood concept is "time is money." We all get it. We are paid a wage to do something; therefore, a value is established. Leftover wages become discretionary income to be spent any way we like. So wasting time is like wasting money. Spend it on something good! When's the last time you thought about it?

And how about the concept of "plan your work, work your plan?" This concept is simple enough. It's straight forward, a no brainer. And therein lies the problem: we don't think about it, and therefore we don't do it!

But these are accepted—even if somewhat untested—and tried-and-true—even if solely in our minds—contemporary concepts nonetheless. They fit nicely into some compartment in the genetically and uninstructed brain. No trial; no error . . . and no gain! My urging to you is to institute the new concepts into your makeup as they are the missing links in going from "error" to "triumph." You must go from the conceptual to the actual. Adopt these concepts so that they become second nature just like supply and demand; time is money; and plan your work, work your plan.

That is not to say that everything should be questioned, but it is to say that everything should be understood if you are to be triumphant in your quest for achievement. Everything you do should be driven by an effort to improve yourself—not fail yourself. Oh, some failure is inevitable, and a small degree of it acts as a learning device of sorts—as long as you analyze and learn from the attempt. But the emphasis of any endeavor should be on a forward push, a winning outcome, a positive prognosis. What sports team takes the field saying, "Let's go out there and lose, guys! After all, we might learn some valuable lessons." Face it, life in general, and especially the business world, just does not work that way.

• • •

The lessons of this entire book are summed up here: Stock your business war chest with the fully-understood and persistently practiced six core concepts that you've been reading about to remove pain before it begins: know what matters, continuously improve, think critically, work thankfully, and plan on being perpetually successful while being competent at what you do. Add in a few thinking systems for good measure to get yourself moving down a gratifyingly triumphant path for personal success.

Also, remember the eight attributes of success from way back at the beginning of the book? They are worth mentioning here again, because, now, having learned the realities of the business world, I'm betting you will see them in a whole new light.

1. Master something; be principled; focus on focusing.

2. Be truly customer centric in the business world but first become egocentric in your personal world.

3. You need not be better than anybody else—just be better tomorrow. Or put another way, if you could have a thought—what would it be?

4. Think and converse in business terms and in business settings by behaving *"businessorally."*

5. Have a business plan in your pocket at all times.

6. Planning without execution is merely an exercise in futility.

7. Work toward securing a sustainable competitive advantage for your business unit; develop a personal sustainable indispensable competency or two for yourself.

8. When it comes to personal and perpetual success, adopt a sense of urgency.

When combined with the concepts and systems that you've been learning throughout this book, these attributes are among the things you don't necessarily learn in college but will serve you well the rest of your business life. Adding them to your repertoire gives you 100 percent of what you need to gain control of your destiny. Curiously delving into them will allow for removal of the intense pain that is associated with being just OK. Ditch that defeatist thinking once and for all and join the ranks of the winners.

• • •

How does this relate to the business world? In this way and with this inquiry: how long can you try and fail at things before the question becomes, how long can you be wrong and remain employed? By aligning yourself with fundamental, structural concepts and core business attributes that remove pain before it begins. The combination of concepts, systems and attributes gives you the best chance for advancement. They give you the best chance for reaching your true potential. They provide you your best option for experiencing the wholesomeness life has to offer. Notice there is not a mention of the word *survival*. Purposely. Because having a purposeful posture eliminates that nasty idea from consideration.

Now you are about to get into an elevator. Are you ready to talk about your business? Do you have the proverbial parachute at the ready?

It was stressed early on in these pages that learning comes from everywhere, starting with the kitchen table. All you have to do to learn is let your ears do the learning for you. Oh, you will have to work and continually get better at it. You'll need to plot and plan as well. Knowing what matters to yourself and your team is foundational. It helps to be principled and competent too.

Going from trial and error to trial and triumph is a posture worth adopting. The former position is like planning to fail. Trial and error is the epitome of a defeatist attitude, as if to say, oh well I'll try this and if it is wrong then I will try that. Those climbing Mount Everest surely expend brain power into where to place the next spike on the vertical wall of ice. Be assured they are not thinking that if it is wrong they'll get up from a 5,000 foot slip, brush themselves off and start again! Would that really remove the pain? Is that how you negotiate the fork in the road or dare I say the forked road in the eight foot by ten foot elevator car?

But that is precisely how many careers are managed—or should I say, mismanaged. I believe it is an entitlement philosophy that permeates the subconscious. How did it get there? Was there brain space left over by not enough concepts filling up the spheres? Nobody owes you anything—just ask the commissioned sales people of the world. You have to work at your career!

Throughout this book I have revealed observed, learned, practiced, enacted, and executed efficacious activities that have led me to believe that trying to be triumphant was better than trying to fail! The best way to remove failure from the trial-and-error equation is to not think about error in the first place. The best way to remove erring is not to try to error! Trial and triumph. It's an attitude that equals altitude. It is a mindset or *Purposeful Posture*. As entrepreneur, author, and speaker on business, motivation and human potential, Tim Fargo, so very rightly points out, doing something wrong repeatedly does not make it right!

• • •

The top three things Pop never failed at were, above all, being Pop; knowing that if the effort was worthy he would be better for having endured it; and being a father.

So, my fatherly advice:

- Nightly relive each day's events, seeking any kind of learning that will help you to grow. *Don't try it—do it.*

- Create a sustainable competitive advantage for the business. Create a personal indispensable competency for yourself. *Don't try it—do it.*

- Adopt the five core principles of the essence of continuous improvement by creating a constancy of purpose towards improvement and adopting new philosophies. Improve constantly and forever by instituting education and self-improvement. Make transformation job number one. *Don't try it—do it.*

- Think, behave and converse "businessorally." *Don't try it—do it.*

- Think even when it hurts. *Don't try it—do it.*

- Are you questioning answers? *Don't try it—do it.*

- Work like you are on commission. *Don't try it—do it.*

- Communicate, navigate, and illuminate via principles. *Don't try it—do it.*

- Urgently pursue your personal and perpetual success. *Don't try it—do it.*

Finally, let's converse about using the art of conversation to attain lofty goals in your business life. You are about to get into another one of those "elevator" situations. I'm sure you are ready to talk about your business!

10

The Conversation
Spoken

"More of your conversation would infect my brain."

William Shakespeare, Coriolanus

As I reached for the overhead bin to collect my obligatory business ammunition consisting of cell phone, laptop, logoed cap, ID card, and passport I caught a glimpse of Hal. This time I was ready.

His initials had grown from EVP to CEO. His hair color now matched his steely gray eyes. The smile now belonged to him. I remembered him from the curdling oatmeal breakfast we abruptly shared some time ago in the concrete jungle. I felt he expected more from me this time. "Hal" to me had become a pseudo-synonym for "How's business," a question I had struggled with for sixty seconds once upon a time in an elevator. Yes, the experience had become personal.

All Hal had to do was nod as if to say, "*continue.*" This time the meal was serenely in its proper place and now instead of lamely responding with "good," I calmly orated this:

Market share and profits are up over last quarter; flat year-to-date as we are now positioned to make a run at our fourth consecutive positive year. Cash flows are north of projections due in part to recent price increases in major brand categories while suffering no discernable fall off in consumer pull. Most analysts' reviews are positive; however, one newcomer remains skeptical. The switch to the broker distribution system is still unclear as one-time charges are yet to flush out of the system voiding year-to-year comparisons.

Our aim is to break the established four-year record, but we temper our expectations depending on currency adjustments in the European Zone. Crop harvest, while always a question, lingers heavily early on in the quarter and thus the big question affecting year-end results.

We have modified our plan to include trade spending targeted to high volume accounts and will monitor this initiative along with the five ongoing programs underway in Q4.

This new plan will require reworking trade spending on the fly to match competitive thrusts. It will entail quick reporting and will be a true test of the new distribution system. We will source finance personnel from the western division as they have experienced this tactic a few years ago. All unit managers have made this priority number one.

Key metrics similar to last year's western test are in place and augmented by the critical factors of holiday preorders and cash flow attainment by region.

Right now the first projection is trending positive. Account managers are meeting the lone holdout account this week. Analyst meetings are set for next week as financial and market share trends are being readied by the finance team. Mid-quarter results will be posted to your dashboard by the end of the month.

In the sixty seconds it took us to reach the jetway, I must have made an impression. Offering me a ride to what I assumed to be the office, Hal had the Town Car driver turn right on Sixty-third Street and a left on Second Avenue to his personal brownstone residence in mid-block. We took the elevator to the penthouse; he offered coffee. He motioned to the kitchen table and simply asked, "What have you learned today, Son?"

Redemption.

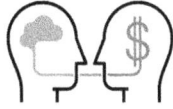

Epilogue

My deep desire has been to pass on my learnings from the kitchen table on up to the hallowed halls of corporate life in the business mecca of the world–Manhattan. I believed college classroom teaching would have been the best place to pass on what I had learned. Much to my chagrin, I was told I didn't have the qualifications to teach at the collegiate level, for I had no published works of merit. I lacked a PhD for God's sake. What audacity to think I could share learning without those two things! It was not good enough that I had developed learning centers for a Fortune 10 company and that for the last thirty-five years I worked and lacked the time to pursue more formal education. In the eyes of the learned faculty of higher education I was just not good enough. I guess Pop wasn't either. Now that I am a published author, can I teach?

A final thought. Don't be afraid to talk out loud at your kitchen table. I have done it for years with my sons. I am surprised and forever thankful for how much they taught me! Your kids may think you're nuts until such time as they venture into the business world, and then they will perhaps unintentionally tell your ears to listen to what they have learned. Their conversation may go like this: "Remember when we were having hot dogs at the baseball game and I laughed at you because the mustard dripped out of the corner of your mouth as you told me about Hal? Well, Pop, just the other day while in a cab our SVP asked me about my business and I top-lined it for him in a New York minute. It was the best cab ride of my life!"

I would love to hear from you and learn how you are passing on your learnings. It is my belief that you can only do so after you apply them yourself, as only then will they have true meaning. Feel free to reach out to me at doofylaturk@gmail.com.

You see a lot of question marks in this book, probably a record of some sort or another! My aim was to draw reactions out of you, conclusions, and notions about what is possible and doable for yourself. Sure, I have provided some insight into the corporate world as I have lived it and it acts as my foundation. However, it only serves to provide context—the real lessons lie in understanding the basic operating principles contained herein. I believe the answers are within you—perhaps you just needed the right questions?

I am not the smartest guy in the world, nor do I proclaim to be. In fact, I have long maintained and understood this about myself:

Epilogue

ABOUT BEING SMART

If I was smart I would have been a failure.

Why, you ask?

Because I probably wouldn't have worked so hard. I probably would not have learned to focus on what was important. I probably wouldn't have challenged myself. I probably would have waited for good things to happen to me.

If I was smart, I probably would have ended up not knowing how smart I was.

By not being innately smart I was forced to become smart. I got the benefit of starting from the bottom. I am still climbing the smart ladder.

I feel smarter now than I ever could have been if I was smart.

I know I am smarter for having written this book. I leave you with this final question: Are you smarter for having read it?

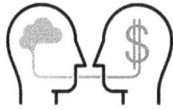

Appendix

1. Example of the 6 Step TPS Process—Thinking,
    Presenting, Selling

    FRAME OF REFERENCE:

    Writing a Non-Fiction Business Book

THE SITUATION:

From Bloomberg Business, written by Eric Spitznagel on
7.9.2012:

*   Publishers keep cranking out as many as 11,000 new
    business books each year, according to the co-authors of
    The 100 Best Business Books of All Time, which doesn't
    account for the untold number of self-published e-books.
    Publishers don't seem to have any idea what works. The

strategy, if it can be called that, is to flood the market and hope a book floats to the surface. So for every *Tipping Point* or *Freakonomics,* there are remainder bins filled with titles such as *Leadership Secrets of Attila the Hun.*

- "I don't read business books," says Nassim Nicholas Taleb, author of *The Black Swan,* a business book that spent thirty-six weeks on the *New York Times* bestseller list. "And I almost never talk to anyone who reads them." He isn't alone in his disdain. "I usually tell people not to read business books at all," says Bob MacDonald, who's written several popular business titles such as *Cheat to Win* and *Beat the System.* "They're just ego trips. You're not going to learn anything."

- *Know the Bountiful Beauty of Brevity.* Peter Drucker's 1974 classic of management literature, *Management: Tasks, Responsibilities & Practices* ran to 839 pages. "It used to be, whoever wrote the biggest book won," says Michael Levin, ghostwriter, author of more than 100 books, and a regular guest on ABC's *Shark Tank.* No longer. "There's nobody today who would read an 800 page Drucker book unless it was on the final exam at a business school."

- So *what's the ideal length?* Kenneth Blanchard, co-author of bestsellers such as *The One Minute Manager* and *Who Moved My Cheese?* suggests 100 pages or less. "When we first shopped around *One Minute Manager* in the early 1980s, nobody in New York would touch us," he remembers. "Everyone was like, 'Who's going to pay $15 for a book that's 100 pages and most of its white space?'" As it turns out, quite a few: 13 million, if you go by Blanchard's website; 539,000, according to Nielsen BookScan.

- "There are *three types of successful business books*," says Jack Covert, a co-author of *The 100 Best Business Books of All Time*. "The first kind is essentially self-help books. And then there's the very hands-on 'How to write a great résumé' type of book. And then there's the linear Malcolm Gladwell kind of book that takes a big research-based idea and tells brilliant stories to support it."

- It's all about what you call it, says Bob MacDonald— "When *Cheat to Win* came out there was more discussion about the title than the content."

- Jim Cramer of CNBC says "Write what you want to read."

Changing Mix of What Sells in Print-Jonathan Nowell, Nielsen Book, 1.15.2015:

- Nonfiction sales are 41 percent of the 635 million books sold—down 5 points over 10 years. Business non-fiction sales are relatively flat over the same period.

- E-book growth is undeniable. Key vendors are Amazon. com (67 percent of all eBooks), Apple, Barnes & Noble, and KOBO I.

The 10 Awful Truths About Book Publishing—Steven Piersanti, President of Berrett-Koehler Publishers, 1.15.2014:

- U.S. book publishing marketplace fell to $27.1 billion.

- According to Nielsen BookScan of January 6, 2014— which tracks most bookstore, online, and other retail sales of books (including Amazon.com)—adult non-fiction print unit book sales peaked in 2007 and have declined every year since then. Only 225 million books were sold in 2013 in the U.S. in all adult nonfiction categories combined (Publishers Weekly, January 6, 2014). The average U.S. nonfiction book is now selling less than 250 copies per year and less than 2,000 copies over its lifetime. And very few titles are big sellers. Only 62 of 1,000 business books released in 2009 sold more than 5,000 copies, according to an analysis by the Codex Group (*New York Times*, March 31, 2010).

- According to the Bowker Report of October 2013 over 391,000 books were self-published books in 2012; an increase of 422 percent from 2007. Annually 700,000 books are published and since 2007, nearly 10 million previously published books have been reissued by companies that reprint public domain works. Unfortunately, the marketplace is not able to absorb all these books, and it is hugely oversaturated.

- A partial strategy to avert the ten awful truths about book publishing: Front-load main ideas in books and keep them short and build books around a big new idea. Even still, the facts are un-deniable . . . a book has less than a 1 percent chance of being stocked in an average bookstore and the average new book generates only $50,000 to $150,000 in sales.

- In his book, *The Business Book Bible*, Derek B. Lewis states "to be considered a success, a business books need to sell 5,000 copies."

Appendix

Other research:

- TechNavio's forecast for the US e-book market will grow 21 percent from 2013 to 2018. Forrester Research, Inc. claims e-book sales will reach $2.81 billion in 2015.

- On average, fewer than 100 hardcover nonfiction bestsellers in any year sell more than 100,000 copies and usually only one or two top 1 million sold. Two thirds of these books are self-published books.

- Says Barbara Monteiro, who runs her New York public-relations firm that specializes in business books, "You have to be part of the conversation. And that means being on Twitter or Facebook." You'll know you're ready when a publisher will put your face on the book jacket.

THE BIG QUESTION(S), IDEA(S) or ISSUE(S)

GENERAL QUESTIONS:

- Is there a need for another nonfiction business book? Is there an audience for it?

- Do I have the patience and time for the demands of the attempt?

- Where could I get help in writing, editing, formatting and cover design?

- Could I stomach the reviews?

- What is the investment; what is the break-even point?

BIG ISSUES:

- Marketing: understand who, what, where, and when.

- Publishing: Learn about self-publishing, vanity publishing, e-publishing.

- Investment: Establish a budget. Answer the monetary question: Do I care about making money/losing money? What is the real reward for me?

IDEA:

Having learned so many lessons from my father, colleagues, peers, subordinates, bosses, clients, and others, and after having numerous business conversations with my three sons and anyone else who may have asked, how about a quick hitting, shorter rather than longer "self-help/ how-to" type book called *Fatherly Business Conversations*?

The Plan:

Background: I was thinking about writing a business book in an effort to pass on my learnings to aspiring and next-generation business moguls. After experiencing a career with increasing responsibilities in top tier companies and varying localities in different industries and after countless conversations and discussions with talented, inspiring, and commanding people, I thought the newest generation of future leaders could stand to learn from it all. I, in effect, was also one of those inspired people, as my resume attests. Put it all together and the makings of a book began to be believable. I had many questions. I had many answers. I had more questions. I had to think about writing, and that hurt so much that I had to learn to think even when it hurts.

In deciding upon the nature of the book, in my reflection stage I casually thought how I learned about business and how a recent college graduate or any young professional may have been prepared for future business challenges. (I was once a recent college graduate too.)

Being in both circumstances at far different times, I thought about how much I learned after college and how much I learned before college. I also had a long and heartfelt conversation with myself and my recently deceased dad about fundamental business traits and not necessarily modern business concepts. I discovered that what set me up for business was not necessarily what I learned in college but what I heard and saw in the early years before I even knew a business world existed. It was those early lessons that shaped who I am and who each of us is. It really does matter to all of us.

And, much to my happy surprise, I reflected on how much I learned from professors, peers, and people from almost every corner in the business world. I was shocked how much I did not know or necessarily grasp in college. I felt it probably wasn't even possible to learn some of the post-college lessons as I was too young and inexperienced to have any perspective. If I did hear or see it, I would not have possibly been able to grasp the essence of it. It wasn't the fault of the college system, it was just the marriage of two worlds that sometimes don't collide until later on in life.

I reasoned that an inherent gap existed in the narrow field of general business knowledge for the liberal arts or nonspecific majors. Heck, I reasoned that if the book addressed fundamental operating principles, then everyone could benefit from the book. Why not?

Interviewing, resume writing, conversational intelligence, and so on was woefully in demand, even though most colleges make it available to some degree. But, who at twenty-something has the perspective to get "it"? I felt if I could traverse the business world to pretty good heights, anybody could do it. After all, I was accepted into college as a "special student" meaning that I had to prove myself in the first semester or think about another avenue for my life! For students like me a peek into the real business world was the farthest thing from our minds.

However, we all catch up eventually, and I felt that a glimpse into the actual corporate world would enlighten and assist one in his preparations for a career—a rewarding one at that! I felt that if a person knew what he was about to embark upon that he would stand a better chance for success. If one could understand how the business world works relative to personal business dealings, he might start off in the right direction and leapfrog his career a few steps. I mused about what a book of this nature would look like while rhetorically questioning if one could benefit from dissecting topics not patently germane to his major but to his performance on the business battlefield?

The questions kept coming; the answers kept saying yes. The doubts kept coming also. The self-confidence ebbed. The challenge of entering into a totally new field was daunting yet exciting. Could I write it? Who would read it? Who cares?

The landscape for books of this nature seemed to be small if nonexistent. There are many "how to" books and ample self-help books, and they are written by some pretty good people. I've read a lot of them myself. Again, I ponder: me, an author . . . who cares?

I needed to figure it out and then it hit me: why not complete the six-step learning process I had used so often in business situations and see where the analysis leads me?

And this, in essence, after understanding the situation with all its questions and possibilities, with all it trappings and possible jubilations is the PLAN—an e-book, softcover and possibly hardcover book entitled:

Fatherly Business Conversations—*The Concepts and Systems You Don't Necessarily Learn in College but Serve You Well the Rest of Your Business Life.*

HOW THE PLAN WORKs:

1. Write an outline. Gather research information. Select the topics/chapters. Stick to what I know. Leave ego at the door; look for new aspiring writer friends.

2. Begin writing to see if the words flow naturally. Find my voice. Set the tone. Establish a pace. Adopt this mantra: Strive for conviction; avoid confliction.

3. Seek advice from trusted friends, business associates, and writing professionals. Read reference materials, scour blogs, establish checkpoints.

4. Learn relevant writing processes and welcome *iteration.*

5. Understand the elements involved in writing, editing and formatting, proofreading, and copywriting a nonfiction book.

6. Learn about the principles of cover design, marketing, and publishing.

7. Write and rewrite. Edit and reedit. Test and retest the ideas. Keep asking if this is a book that someone would read, learn from, and ultimately enjoy?

8. Follow this plan; make it iterative.

Action	Who	What	Where	When
PHASE 1				
Writing	Author & a co-writer?	Short, fast paced non-fiction book	Home Office	Start March 2012
Editing/ Ghost Writing?	Professional	Developmental, substantive & copy editing	Virtual	Early on & continuing
Proofreading	Professional	Line by line	Virtual	Mid & post completion
Checkpoint #1	Author(s)	Go/no-go?	Gut Check	Upon Phase 1 completion
PHASE 2	Who	What	Where	When
Layout Formatting	Professional	From prologue to epilogue & more. Easy reading flow	Virtual	Post writing
Copyright	Author	Ownership Protection	USCO	Upon Phase 1 completion
Book Formatting	Professional	Hard/softcover & all electronic versions	Virtual	Post layout
Cover Design	Professional	Impactful	Virtual	After check #1
Checkpoint #2	Author(s)	Go/no-go?	Gut Check	Upon Phase 2 completion

Appendix

PHRASE 3	Who	What	Where	When
Secure ISBN's	Author	Unique identifier	Bowker	Only if a "go"
Book Reviewed	Readers, writers & professionals	Honest feedback for final go/no-go	Virtual	Prior to marketing & publishing
Marketing	Author and/or professional	Separate detailed plan with/without profit motive	Author/ Agency?	Explore after checkpoint #1
Publishing	Self-publish vs. vanity publishing	Address the profit question; conduct break/ even analysis?	Author/ agency	Constant education/ Careful consideration

HOW TO MEASURE SUCCESS:

Success will largely be based upon completing the manuscript as it is not uncommon for writers, especially newbies, to give up on the quest. Greater success will depend on positive reviews and eventually sales if that route is taken. Lastly, I will consider leaving the reader with an email address to contact me with their experiences. The nature and volume of responses may outweigh potential monetary results.

Penultimate success would be a listing of *Fatherly Business Conversations* among "The First Five Books for Those New to Business" as recorded by 800-CEO-READ Bestsellers. The ultimate reward would be a mention on The 100 Best Business Books of All Time presented at the annual 800-CEO-READ

Business Book Awards. Finally, perpetual success can be defined by increasing sales volume and the readership's robust desire for Fatherly Business Conversations 2.0.

Metric	Measurement	Notes
Completed Manuscript	Written according to the Chicago Style	3–4 years
Phase 1	Go/No go Checkpoint #1	Q2 2015
Phase 2	Go/No go Checkpoint #2	Q4 2015
Phase 3	Go/No go Checkpoint #3	Q1 2016
Reviews	Target Positive vs. Negative ratio >75%	Q2 2016
Sales Volume (dollars)	Medium of non-fiction is apx. $100,000	2017/18
Hard Cover book sales volume	Top 25% of non-fiction equals apx. 40,000 copies	2018/19

IMMEDIATE NEXT STEPS:

Write, write, write; edit, edit, edit. Write some more; edit some more.

Concurrently, keep an eye out for possible editors, layout and cover designers, publishers, and marketers.

Learn the business of writing, marketing, and publishing a nonfiction book all in an effort to make an informed decision relative to checkpoint #1.

Seek inspiration by having a heartfelt conversation with my father.

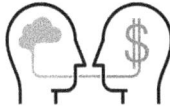

Bibliography

Alef, Daniel. *Clarence W. Barron: Founder of Modern Financial Journalism.* Santa Barbara, CA: Titans of Fortune Publishing, Kindle Edition, 2010.

Apple Watch. San Francisco, CA: The Wikimedia Foundation, 2015.

Bardwick, Judith M. *Danger in the Comfort Zone.* New York, NY: Amacom, 1995.

Belniak, Alan. *The Differences between Goals, Objectives, Strategy, and Tactics.* www.subjectivelyspeaking. net/2013/12/03/the-differences-between-goals-objectives-strategy-and-tactics. Subjectively Speaking, 2013.

Buscaglia, Leo F. *Loving Each Other*. New York, NY: The Random House, 1984.

Business Strategy: Execution Is the Key. ftpress.com. FT Press financial Times. New Jersey: Pearson Education, 2016.

Capra, Fritjof. *The Turning Point: Science, Society, and the Rising Culture*. New York, NY: Simon and Schuster, 1982.

Celsi, Claire. *How to Differentiate Goals, Objectives, Strategies, and Tactics*. www.prdaily.com/Main/Articles/How_to_ differentiate_goals_objectives_strategies_a_16995.aspx. Ragan's PR Daily, 2014.

Chen, Brian X. *Changing Tactics, Apple Promotes Watch as a Luxury Item*. New York Times, 2015.

Clarence W. Barron. San Francisco, CA: The Wikimedia Foundation, 2015.

Deming, W. Edwards. *Out of Crisis*. Cambridge: MIT Center for Advanced Educational Services, 1994.

Deming, W. Edwards. *The DEMING Management Method*. New York, NY: The Berkley Publishing Group, 1986.

Difference Between Goals and Strategies. differencebetween. net/business/difference-between-goals-and-strategies. Differencebetween.net, 2016.

Earnings Estimate. investopedia.com. Investopedia. New York, NY: InterActiveCorp, 2015.

Earnings Per Share—EPS. investopedia.com. Investopedia. New York: InterActiveCorp, 2015.

Bibliography

Fargo, Tim. *Alphabet Success: Keeping it Simple—My Secrets to Success.* St. Petersburg: CreateSpace Independent Publishing Platform, 2014.

Ghanbari, Meysam. *Business Goals vs. Objectives vs. Strategies vs. Tactics.* www.linkedin.com/pulse/20140616055721-142774715-business-goals-vs-objectives-vs-strategies-vs-tactics, 2014.

Hom, Elaine J. *Steve Jobs Biography.* www.businessnewsdaily.com/4195-business-profile-steve-jobs.html. Business News Daily, 2013.

Iacocca, Lee. *Where Have All the Leader Gone?* New York, NY: Scribner, 2008.

Isaacson, Walter. *Steve Jobs.* New York, NY: Simon & Schuster, 2013.

Lewis, Derek B. *The Business Book Bible: Everything You Need to Know to Write a Great Business Book.* Derek Lewis, LLC; 1 edition, 2014.

Manjoo, Farhad. *Apple Watch Review: Bliss, but Only After a Steep Learning Curve.* New York Times, 2015.

Moon, Brad. *Apple Watch: What Can We Really Expect?* InvestorPlace.com. Rockville, MD, 2015.

New World Encyclopedia contributors. *Clarence W. Barron.* Chicago: New World Encyclopedia, 2012.

Pereira, Cliffton. *Marketing- Analysis of Apple Watch.* www.academia.edu/11141073/Marketing-_Analysis_of_Apple_Watch, University of Kent, UK, 2015.

Rohn, Jim. *My Philosophy For Successful Living*. Melrose: No Dream Too Big Publishing, 2012.

Sprague, Edwin J. *The Z Factor*. New Jersey: Career Press, 2013.

360-degree feedback. en.wikipedia.org. Wikipedia. San Francisco: The Wikimedia Foundation, 2015.

Welch, Jack. *Winning*. New York, NY: Harper Collins, 2005.

Index

Index

Index

Work
  attitudes about, 49–50
  commission approach,
    51–52
  energy and, 52
  focusing and, 55–57

mastery, 53
planning and, 51
principles and, 54–55

Z

The Z Factor (Sprague), 54